Inequality & Personal Income Taxes

The Mirage of Progressive Tax Rates in the United States

By Michael D. Williams

Copyright © 2020 by Michael D. Williams

All rights reserved. No part of this book may be used or reproduced in any manner whatsoever, including Internet usage, without the written permission of the author.

Cover design by Michael D. Williams

Publications in the Inequality Series

This is the second publication in my Inequality series and it deals with personal Income Taxes.

The first, a short study, is titled "U.S. Inequality and Economic Growth: A Call for a Deeper Dive."

Please send me your comments, suggestions, corrections and ideas by email to mwbook@outlook.com.

You can you can learn about my professional background on Linked In at https://www.linkedin.com/in/mweconomics/ and you can learn about my publications on my author page at http://amazon.com/author/mwbook.

Table of Contents

Background & Overview — 7
United States Income Inequality
A Brief History of U.S. Income Tax Legislation
Complexity & Interconnectivity
A Sketch of the U.S. Personal Income
  Tax System

Tax Policy Recommendations — 35
Personal Taxes
Corporate Taxes

Rationale for the Policy Prescriptions — 39

Linking Income Taxes and Inequality — 45
Poverty
Health
Education

Personal Income Tax Basics — 67
The Process for Computing Tax Liability
Computing Long-Term Capital Gains
  [LTCG] Taxes
Computing the Alternative Minimum Tax [AMT]
The Tax Cuts and Job Acts of 2017
Under Reporting Income

Payroll Tax Basics — 95

Business Taxes and Inequality — 101

Historical Perspective — 111

Comparing the Current Tax System with The Proposals   133
Personal Income Taxes
Individual Payroll Taxes
Business Taxes

The Nature of Big Business in the United States   141

Beyond Taxes   155
Minimum Wage
Jobs Program

Conclusions   159

A Note on Methodology   167

Statistical Appendix   171

Bibliography   175

Acknowledgements   203

Background & Overview

United States Income Inequality

Before diving into income taxes, let's take a long-term view of income Inequality in the United States. To measure inequality, a standard metric called the "Gini Coefficient" is used and a plot of the data from 1970 to 2018 is shown below. Inequality today is the highest it has been since 1929 at the time of the great stock market crash.

U.S. Index of Income Inequality: The Gini Coefficient

Source: US Federal Reserve Bank of St. Louis, see https://fred.stlouisfed.org/series/GINIALLRF

The data reveal a steady upward movement in the level of inequality, but does not reflect the sense of despair and frustration of many in the lowest income groups. At the end of May 2020, the United States experienced protesting and riots on a scale not seen for decades.

8 | Background & Overview

What happened to cause these riots? The coronavirus pandemic hit the U.S. in March 2020 and by the end of May 2020 about 40 million people had lost their jobs and over a 100,000 people had died from the virus. Of those that died, over 20% had lost their jobs while already living close to poverty. These were the working poor. Studies discovered a disproportionate number of those that were infected and died were from poor minorities. Concurrently, white police officers in various jurisdictions continued to kill black people without good reason. The riots ensued. As Kareem Abdul-Jabbar said in an Opinion article in the *Los Angeles Times* on May 30, 2020, "What you should see when you see black protesters in the age of Trump and coronavirus is people pushed to the edge, not because they want bars and nail salons open, but because they want to live. To breathe."

This built-up frustration is not going away. Unless the trajectory of this inequality indicator changes dramatically in the near term, the United States could be in for more civil unrest. The country needs to focus on the real economy – not stock prices.

A Brief History of U.S. Income Tax Legislation

There are many factors that drive income inequality but this study will examine the linkages between U.S. income inequality and the U.S. income tax code – with the focus on individual taxes. Shown below are the highest marginal individual U.S. income tax rates and the lowest individual U.S. income tax rates.

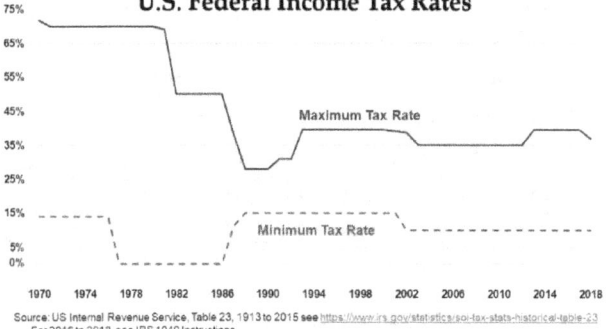

The period on the chart covers 49 years from 1970 to 2018 including the beginning year and the ending year. During that time, the maximum tax rate decreased nine [9] times, increased three [3] times and remained unchanged for 36 years. By contrast, the minimum tax rate decreased three [3] times, increased one [1] time, and remained unchanged for 44 years. This means that the maximum tax rate is three times as likely to decrease as the minimum tax rate and the maximum tax rate is three times as likely to increase as the minimum tax rate. The minimum tax rate tends to be more stable as there are fewer annual changes.

A brief review of some tax legislation:

- **The Tax Reform Act of 1969** was signed into law by President Nixon and its largest impact was creating the Alternative Minimum Tax or AMT, which was intended to obtain revenue from wealthy tax payers who avoided income tax through certain exemptions or deductions. The Act also increased taxes over several years on long term capital gains greater than $50,000 to 35% from 25%.

- **The Tax Reform Act of 1976** was signed into law by President Ford. Included in this Act was increasing the holding period for capital gains to qualify as Long-Term Capital Gains to one year from six months.

- **The Economic Recovery Tax Act of 1981** was signed into law by President Reagan and was the first piece of tax legislation known as the Reagan tax cuts. This legislation contained the largest tax cuts in

U.S. history. The biggest tax cuts were for wealthy Americans, which reduced the maximum tax rate to 50% from 70%; the minimum tax rate was reduced to 11% from 14%; and the Long-Term Capital Gains [LTCG] tax rate was reduced to 20% from 28%. These tax cuts were phased in over several years and amplified income inequality by providing disproportionate benefits to the wealthy. In addition, income brackets were indexed to inflation. After the passage of this legislation the deficit expanded rapidly while interest rates were soaring and the economy went into another recession. These problems led to the next piece of tax legislation.

- **The Tax Equity and Fiscal Responsibility Act of 1982** was signed by President Reagan and is sometimes referred to as the largest tax increase of the post-war era. Much of the tax reduction from 1981 was undone by this piece of legislation in which planned tax cuts were cancelled before being fully implemented. Mandatory withholding on interest and dividends paid was another aspect of this legislation.

- **The Tax Reform Act of 1986** was signed into law by President Reagan and was the second of two pieces of legislation known as the Reagan Tax Cuts. The top individual tax rate was decreased to 33% from 50% and the Act expanded the earned income tax credit, the standard deduction, personal exemptions and the Alternative Minimum Tax. Under Reagan, the national debt almost tripled.

- **The Omnibus Budget Reconciliation Act of 1993** was signed into law by President Bill Clinton. The bill's aim was to reduce federal deficits which had plagued the country for over a decade. It increased the top individual tax rate to 39.6% from 31%, increased fuel taxes and corporate income taxes and reduced some expenditures. The result was a budget surplus in 1998 – which was the first since the 1960s. The budget surplus continued for several years until the tax cuts of 2001.

- **The Economic Growth and Tax Relief Reconciliation Act of 2001** was signed into law by President George W. Bush. This Act lowered federal income tax rates for all brackets including the top rate which declined to 35% from 39.6%. A new tax bracket of 10% was created at the low end. The Act also increased the standard deduction and increased the amount of

Background & Overview | 13

assets excluded for the estate tax. There was also a "sunset" provision by which the tax cuts were scheduled to end in 2011, however, most of the tax cuts were made permanent by the American Taxpayer Relief Act of 2012. In addition, the Jobs Growth and Reconciliation Act of 2003 [also signed by President Bush] reduced federal revenues by another $350 billion. In 2012, analysis by the Congressional Budget Office stated all the Bush tax cuts reduced federal revenue by $1.2 trillion over 10 years.

- **The Tax Cuts and Jobs Act of 2017** was signed into law by President Donald Trump. The major components of the legislation were reducing individual and business income tax rates. On individual taxes, the personal exemption was eliminated and the standard deduction was increased significantly with limits on itemizing deductions. On the business side, there is a 20% "pass through" for certain business entities such as partnerships and S corporations. The effect of this pass through is to reduce individual income tax liability as the provision reduces taxable income by 20% of the income passed through to the recipient. The General Accountability office found that beyond a temporary boost to the economy in 2018, there was no meaningful difference to families from this legislation. The Congressional Budget Office estimated the Act would add $1.9 trillion in deficits over 10 years, while the Tax Policy Center viewed the legislation as regressive and amplifying inequality because the majority of the benefits accrued to the wealthy.

While this review is brief and not comprehensive, it does highlight what appears to be a trend to reduce individual income tax rates – and the rates at the top were usually reduced the most. To see how the difference between the highest and lowest individual tax rates have changed, the low is subtracted from the high for each year and plotted in the chart below. As you can tell, the difference has contracted substantially since 1970.

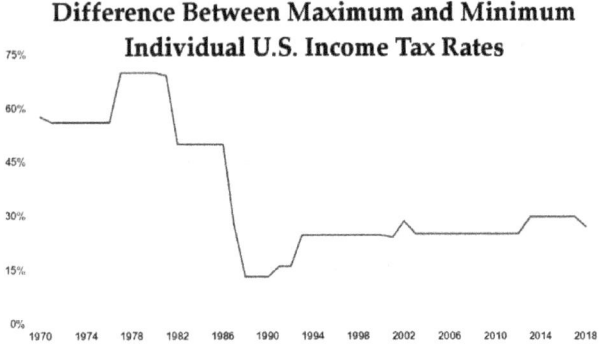

Source: US Internal Revenue Service Table 23, 1913 to 2015 see https://www.irs.gov/statistics/soi-tax-stats-historical-table-23
For 2016 to 2018 see IRS 1040 Instructions

It's also worth it to look at some of the average differences over time. Between 1970 and 1980 the average difference between the maximum tax rate and minimum tax rate was about 56%. Since 2000, the average difference has been about 27%. There are many factors that affect taxes paid that are not included in maximum and minimum tax rates. Some of these factors include the Alternative Minimum Tax or AMT, preferential tax rates for certain categories of income, tax credits, phaseout of itemized deductions, surcharges and more. The more one digs into this topic, the more complex it becomes. As we will learn later in this study, the preferential tax rate on certain categories of income has one of the biggest impacts on the maximum tax rate actually paid by taxpayers.

Complexity & Interconnectivity

The causes of Inequality are complex and interconnected. There is inequality in every social system – the issue is the level of inequality. The chart below shows direct and indirect effects of the level of inequality and the chart is purposely complex in order to highlight the reality. I only provide six topics related to inequality – skills/education, economic growth, health, environment, political influence and poverty. There are other topics affected by inequality, but I have limited the discussion to these six topics to help simplify the matter as much as possible.

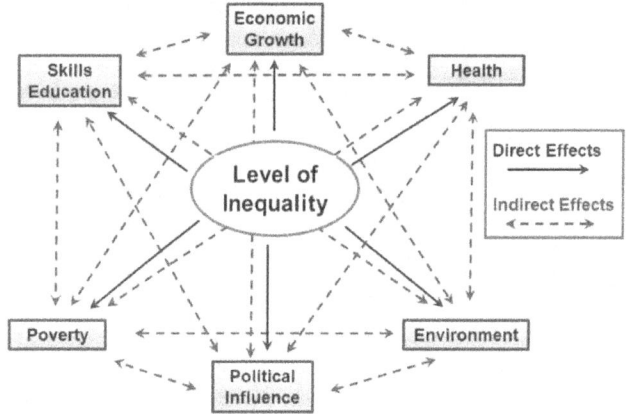

When there is a high level of inequality, economic growth is slower as a larger portion of national income is saved [not spent] because the very wealthy do not spend at the same rate as middle-income and lower-income households. When there is a higher level of inequality, the poorer tend to have less access to health care and job skills that pay lower wages. Both of these things reduce the economic potential of the system. And with greater inequality, those in the upper tiers tend to have more influence on the political system.

In fact, the political system may well be part of the problem as those in the U.S. Congress have a median net worth greater than $1 million, which makes them about ten times wealthier than the net worth of the median U.S. household [see https://qz.com/1190595/the-typical-us-congress-member-is-12-times-richer-than-the-typical-american-household/]. While this is a single blog on the topic, BallotPedia tracks the net worth of our elected officials and has the following table on their website [See https://ballotpedia.org/Net_worth_of_United_States_Senators_and_Representatives.]

Net Worth of U.S. Senators and Representatives

Year	# of Reports	Total Net Worth	Average
2011	627	$4,946,090,771	$7,888,502
2010	641	$4,680,278,853	$7,301,527
2009	652	$4,271,710,652	$6,551,703
2008	600	$3,834,468,090	$6,390,780
2007	603	$4,633,904,377	$7,684,750
2006	594	$3,979,189,252	$6,698,972
2005	542	$3,459,576,717	$6,382,983
2004	580	$3,533,674,470	$6,092,542

Source: BallotPedia, see
ballotpedia.org/Net_worth_of_United_States_Senators_and_Representatives

This table shows an average net worth of about $7.9 million in 2011 for the elected Senators and Congressmen in Washington D.C. The reason the average is so high, is because several of the elected officials are worth more than $100 million – which raises the average, see Business Insider at

https://www.businessinsider.com/how-richest-members-congress-made-money-house-senate-2019-2.

This wealth of our elected officials has come into sharp focus in recent years as the wealthy have promoted – and our elected wealthy officials have passed – tax laws that tend to cater to the wealthy by lowering their taxes while decreasing benefits for the less well off.

In 2019, the Speaker of the House of Representatives had a net worth of about $120 million while the Senate Majority Leader had a net worth over $20 million [see Wikipedia, https://en.wikipedia.org/wiki/List_of_current_members_of_the_United_States_Congress_by_wealth#:~:text=Sen.,the%20wealthiest%20member%20of%20Congress.]

With a higher level of inequality, the indirect effects amplify issues. For example, with higher inequality there is more poverty, which leads to more homelessness, and lower caloric intake, greater susceptibility to sickness and disease, and greater stress on the health care system. With greater homelessness, there is a higher likelihood that homeless children will not attend school, which leads to lower education and skill levels – which impact productivity and economic growth. The interrelationships are broad, complex and deep.

The pandemic of 2020 laid bare health care issues related to inequality. Initial analysis of those that lost their job to the coronavirus pandemic in 2020, reveals that about 39% of those laid off earned less than $40,000 per year. And initial analysis of those that died of coronavirus in May 2020, reveals a disproportionately high rate of death among minorities, groups already experiencing the downside of income inequality due to a number of factors. In April and May of 2020 about 40 million Americans lost their jobs and when they lost their jobs, many lost their health insurance or the ability to pay to for a health insurance plan. It is quite possible that more than 25% of Americans no longer have health insurance in the United States – which puts the U.S. economy at risk.

The 2020 pandemic also reveals the impact of inequality in K-12 education. Most schools across the country were closed during the pandemic. Children of wealthier families had access to the internet and electronic devices so they could continue their education on-line at home. Children of the less well-off did not have these options and their education was halted. Worse, many K-12 students experienced a lack of food since the schools served as a main source of meals for many.

In my first study on income inequality in the U.S., I established that inequality has been increasing in the U.S. for decades and there is a slightly negative relationship between inequality and economic growth, i.e., greater income inequality is associated with slower economic growth. The chart below captures these ideas.

Background & Overview | 21

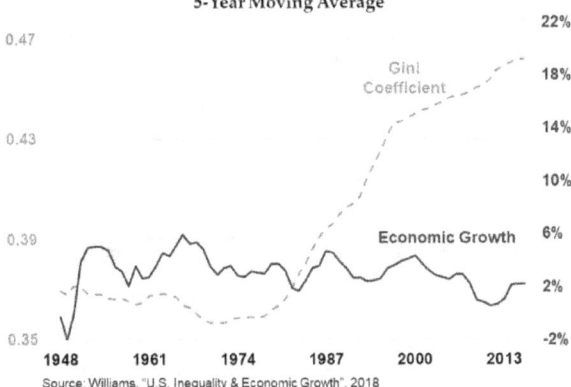

U.S. Gini Coefficient & Economic Growth
5-Year Moving Average

Source: Williams, "U.S. Inequality & Economic Growth", 2018

You can see in the chart that inequality [the dashed green line] – as measured by the Gini coefficient – increases rather consistently after 1974 while economic growth – the solid blue line – goes through its cycles at a lower level than the cycles observed between 1950 and 1975. Much of the household income tax data presented in this study only goes through 2015 because that is the most recent data available, and that is the reason the charts do not go to 2019. This is particularly important as the historical data from the *Tax Cuts and Jobs Act of 2017* are *not* available. In spite of this shortcoming, the key trends have not changed and the recent Tax Act amplifies factors that increase income inequality.

A Sketch of the U.S. Personal Income Tax System

One thing is clear, the current tax system gives the illusion of being progressive, but is far less progressive than advocates would have you believe. In other words, the income tax system in the U.S. helps amplify income inequality by bestowing significant benefits on the wealthy.

The tax chart below is for personal income taxes for 2015 – the most recent years of tax return data available, but before the 2017 Tax Act. This table is for taxable income for a married couple filing a joint return. The horizontal axis contains the income level. For a married couple with taxable income under $18,450, the tax rate is 10%. For a married couple with taxable income between $18,450 and $74,900, the tax rate is 15%. The table continues until taxable income is above $464,850 – and for that income, the tax rate is 39.6%. Thus, you can see the progressive nature of the federal income tax system.

United States Progressive Personal Income Tax Rates

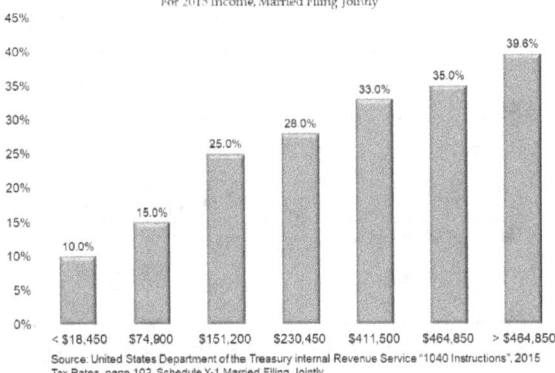

Source: United States Department of the Treasury Internal Revenue Service "1040 Instructions", 2015 Tax Rates, page 102, Schedule Y-1 Married Filing Jointly

Looking at this table, one would expect a married couple with taxable income of about $75,000 would have a tax rate less than 15% since the first $18,450 is taxed at 10% and the remainder is taxed at 15%. The actual tax data released to the public does not match these brackets as the data are presented for quintiles of households, thus, there is not a perfect match between public tax records and tax brackets. In addition, the income presented for the quintiles is total personal income – which is not taxable income and does not include items such as itemized deductions, credits and so forth. In the chart below, the tax rates for the quintiles are presented for 2015.

It now gets much more complicated.

In the income data provided by the US Congressional Budget Office, "Federal Taxes" are composed of two parts:

1. Federal income taxes paid on "taxable income" using the chart above.
2. Payroll taxes paid on "earned income." For 2015, the payroll tax rate for individuals was 7.65% on earned income up to $118,500. Of the 7.65%, 6.2% was allocated to social security and 1.45% was allocated to Medicare.

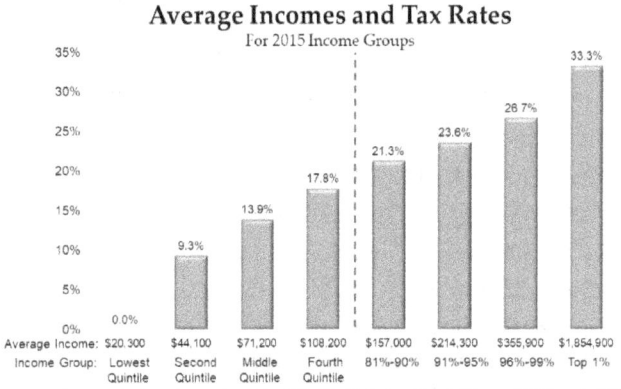

Just reviewing the chart reveals the progressive nature of the federal tax system. As personal income increases, the average tax rate for each quintile increases. At the far left is the lowest income quintile with an average total income [not taxable income] of $20,300 and this quintile has an average federal tax rate of 1.5% [includes income taxes and payroll taxes]. The standard deduction, personal exemptions, credits and subsidies lower personal income significantly and it seems reasonable the income tax rate would be near zero. In 2015 the standard deduction for a married couple filing jointly was $12,600 and the personal exemption was $4,000 per person. For a couple with no children, this translates to $8,000 and the combination of standard deduction and personal exemption takes the taxable income near zero. But payroll taxes are due on all earned income and they are 7.65% of that income. Keep in mind the lowest quintile is composed of millions of households and some are below average and some above average – and, the households have to pay payroll taxes on all earned income. Given the adjustments to income and payroll taxes, the 1.5% tax rate seems reasonable.

At the other end of the spectrum, the top 1% have an average personal income of $1,854,900 – which puts them in the 39.6% tax bracket. Their average income tax rate is 33.3% and we know that their taxable income up to $464,850 is taxed at lower rates. Payroll taxes are only paid on the first $118,500 of earned income which means payroll taxes are only paid on 6.4% of their income. This category of taxpayer likely uses itemized deductions in addition to personal exemptions and credits. Because I thought the 33.3% average tax rate seemed low, I undertook computations making two assumptions: [1] All income was taxed at the tax rate in the tax schedules, and [2] payroll taxes were paid on $118,500 [the maximum taxed in 2015]. Using these two assumptions, the tax rate would be 37.2% - about 12% higher than the average computed by the Congressional Budget Office. My computations do not include deductions or exemptions which would reduce the income tax liability.

One thing that makes this income category different from the lowest quintile is the type of income – which is taxed at lower rates than found in the tax schedule. Top income earners receive income from categories such as interest from tax-free municipal bonds, long-term capital gains [LTCG], carried interest and qualified dividends. The chart below compares the tax rates of long-term capital gains to the highest marginal federal income tax rate.

Background & Overview | 27

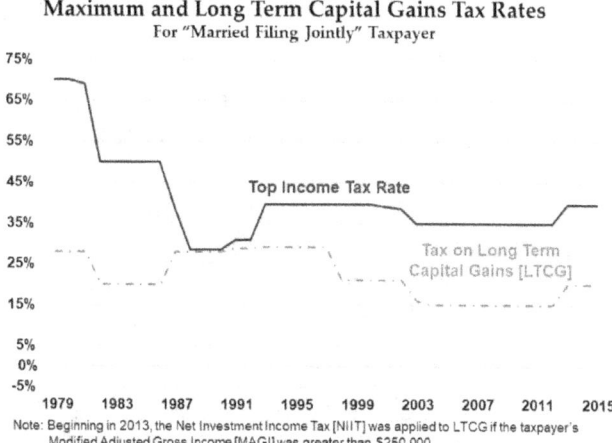

Maximum and Long Term Capital Gains Tax Rates
For "Married Filing Jointly" Taxpayer

Note: Beginning in 2013, the Net Investment Income Tax [NIIT] was applied to LTCG if the taxpayer's Modified Adjusted Gross Income [MAGI] was greater than $250,000
Sources: Congressional Research Service and Tax Foundation

For most of the years between 1979 and 2015, the LTCG tax rate was much lower than the top income tax rate. For 2015 it was almost 20% lower. This tax rate also applied to income categories titled "qualified dividends" and "carried interest." Also in 2015, there was something called the Alternative Minimum Tax or AMT. For people with high incomes, the AMT phases out their deductions so additional income tax would be collected. For people receiving interest from tax-free municipal bonds, it is difficult to estimate the tax rate on their total income without knowing the portion of their income from tax free municipal bonds. As you

28 | Background & Overview

can tell, it is much more complex at the upper income levels.

Because tax free municipal bonds, LTCG, qualified dividends and carried interest are taxed at lower income tax rates than the tax tables, it is instructive to get a sense of the size of these categories of income and learn which income quintiles contain these categories. For this study, these four categories are combined and called "Special Income."

For 2015, Special Income totaled about $1 trillion or about 13% of the $13.2 trillion of Total Personal Income.

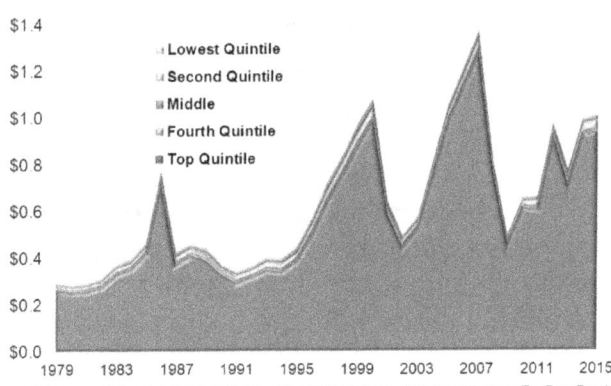

US Special Income*
In Trillions of Constant 2015 US$

* Composed of Long Term Capital Gains, Qualified Dividends, Carried Interest and Tax Free Bonds
Source: U.S. Congressional Budget Office, January 2019

This chart highlights that the level of Special Income varies significantly from year to year and the vast majority of Special Income is obtained by the those in the top quintile – which is the dark blue color. In fact, the top quintile receives more than 90% of the Special Income category. For those in the Top 1%, their share of personal income classified as Special Income was about 13% in 2015. To put this in dollar terms, the average income for the top quintile was about $292,000 and 13% of the total is about $38,000. Just the Special Income of the top quintile is about 80% larger than the average income for the lowest quintile which averaged $20,300 in 2015.

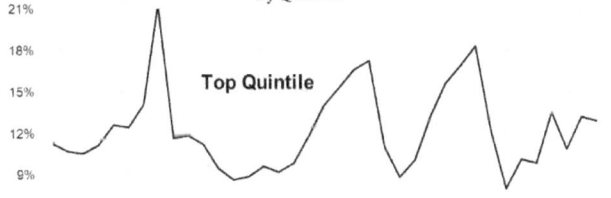

Shares of Household Income from Special Income
By Quintile

Source: U.S. Congressional Budget Office, US Distribution of Household Income 2015, November 2018

We now see a key factor – those at the highest income levels have the opportunity to legally reduce their income tax liability through special sections of the tax code. An examination of the concentration of wealth for the Top 1% reveals they owned just under 40% of all U.S wealth – similar to the share held by the Top 1% just after the stock market crash of 1929.

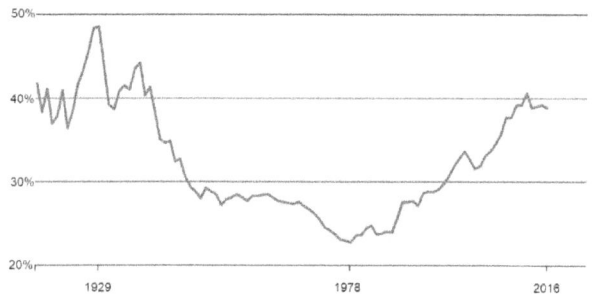

Shares of Household Income Held By Top 1%

Source: U.S. Congressional Budget Office. US Distribution of Household Income 2015. November 2018

To put this wealth concentration into a human perspective, the Institute for Policy Studies estimated that in 2020 Jeff Bezos, Bill Gates and Warren Buffet own as much wealth as the bottom half of all U.S. households. The number of billionaires in the U.S. has grown from 66 in 1990 to 614 in 2020 and their combined wealth has soared from $118.8 billion to $2.95 trillion during the same time period. In the U.S. wealth has become much more concentrated over the last 30 years [see "Billionaire Bonanza," 2020] with an increase in inequality.

And if we examine the wealth shares for all the income groups, we see the top 10% dominates owning about 70% of assets in 2013. The volumes and shares change over time as asset prices increase and decrease. The key point is that the top quintile owns the vast majority of wealth in the United States and has the opportunity to pay favorable tax rates on the income from this wealth.

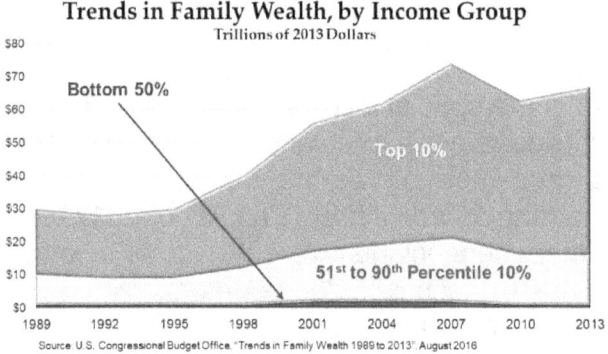

The average tax rate for the top income brackets has varied over the last few decades, but is still lower than the tax rates in the 1950s when the highest marginal rate was greater than 90%. Changes to the tax code and changes to payroll taxes have caused some of the variation. Taxpayer ingenuity with different categories of income is also an area ripe for gaming the system.

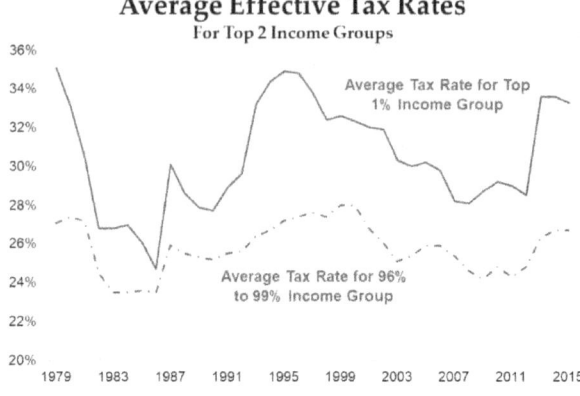

Source: United States Congressional Budget Office, "The Distribution of Household Income 2015", November 2018.

And if the special interest groups think the top tax rates are still too high, they can lobby their congressmen to lower the tax rates – and this is what happened with the Tax Act of 2017 whose primary beneficiaries were the upper income groups – which included senators, congressmen and the president. According to the Center on Budget and Policy Priorities [CBPP], about 27% of the tax benefits from the Tax Act of 2017 went to the Top 1% income group. Another 59% of the benefits went to the next 39% of households. And the remaining 14% of benefits from the Tax Act of 2017 went to the remaining 60% of households. The benefits were not spread evenly among all income quintiles and thus, the Tax Act of 2017 amplified income inequality. The graphic below highlights these statistics.

Background & Overview | 33

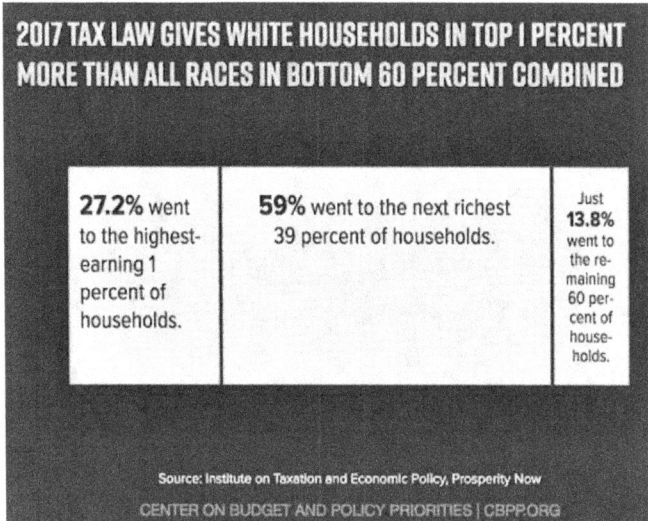

Apart from lower tax rates for the upper tiers, the Tax Act of 2017 also allowed taxpayers to reduce their "pass-through income" by 20%, thereby lowering their taxable income by 20% which lowered their tax liability by 20%. This pass-through income is for self-employment, partnerships, Limited Liability Companies [LLC] and certain categories of asset income such as income mortgage real estate investment trusts [mREIT].

Tax Policy Recommendations

The recommendations presented in this study were created by me and are divided into two broad categories: Personal Taxes and Corporate Taxes. The underlying emphasis in creating these recommendations is to reduce income inequality, broaden the tax base, simplify the tax code, and eliminate preferential tax treatment. Each recommendation is now highlighted.

Personal Taxes

- **Income Categories** – All income should be taxed at the same rate. There should not be preferential income tax rates for carried interest, long term capital gains, qualified dividends and interest from tax-free municipal bonds.
- **Standard Deduction** – increase by 50%.
- **Itemized Deductions** – eliminate.
- **Alternative Minimum Tax** – eliminate.
- **Payroll Taxes** – should be applied to all non-earned income as they are applied to earned income. The difference: there will be no "employer contribution" for payroll taxes on non-earned income.
- **Top Tax Rate** – increase to 40%.

Administrative Matters for Personal Income Taxes

- **Calendar Year Basis** – all income reported to individuals by investment firms should be done so on a cash, not accrual basis. This change would apply primarily to non-earned income.
- **1099s** – For BOTH earned and non-earned income should be mailed to individuals no later than the end of January.
- **Fourth Quarterly Payment** – should be due February 14.

Corporate Taxes

- **Twenty Percent Exclusion** from the 2017 Tax Act – eliminate.
- **Interest Expense Deductions** – eliminate.
- **Depreciation Expenses** – eliminate.
- **Capital Investments Expenses** – deduct in the year of the investment.
- **Corporate Tax Incentives** – eliminate.
- **Alternative Minimum Tax** – eliminate.
- **Loss Carryover** – limit the number of years that losses can be carried forward to one.
- **Maximum Corporate Tax Rate** – remain at 21%.

The remainder of this book outlines my justification for these recommendations, and outlines the manner in which implementing these changes will work to close the income inequality gap.

Rationale for the Policy Prescriptions

The guiding principles for my recommendations are derived from the preamble to the

> *We the People of the United States, in Order to form a more perfect Union, establish Justice, insure domestic Tranquility, provide for the common defence, **promote the general Welfare**, and secure the Blessings of Liberty to ourselves and our Posterity, do ordain and establish this Constitution for the United States of America.*

constitution that states:

My focus as it relates to inequality is "promote the general welfare." To **promote the general welfare** implies U.S. citizens are [1] healthy and [2] economically productive – which implies having work skills. These are the keys to a vibrant population that can help the United States prosper.

Income inequality has ramifications for our country's well-being and economic prosperity. Productivity is a measure of output per person and sustained long-term economic growth comes from increases in productivity. The greater the productivity, the greater the output.

More rapid increases in productivity implies faster economic growth and a higher standard of living as employees are producing more per hour and receive higher inflation adjusted wages.

Productivity is often associated with technological innovation. However, the key to increased productivity is humans – they are the ones that create the technology and manage the machines that can be used to improve productivity. In the U.S. in 2019, the unemployment rate was below 4% and it was challenging for employers to find people with skills matching their labor needs. People had skills but not those in high demand, which I believe is the result of people not having the ability to finance the needed education to obtain the skills.

In 2017 in the U.S., households in the top 10% income group spent 47% of all household expenditures on education. The top 10% spent more than the lower 80% and the people in the top 10% had opportunities not available to those in the lower 80%. Annual post-high school education costs in the U.S. have been growing rapidly over the last decade leaving the advanced level of education easiest to obtain by those in the upper income brackets.

Rationale for the Policy Prescriptions | 41

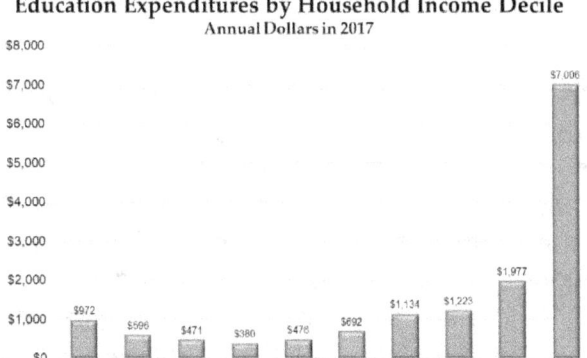

Education Expenditures by Household Income Decile
Annual Dollars in 2017

Source: Bureau of Labor Statistics, Consumer Expenditure Survey, released September 2018.

Further amplifying inequality, the 339 public universities in the United States distributed about 40% of their aid budgets on students the federal government deemed able to afford their education who did not need the aid, in other words, the more affluent students. The transformation in providing aid to non-needy students comes about because state governments have reduced funding to public universities. To cope with the loss of income, universities seek out-of-state students and provide aid to the "best and the brightest" state residents – who are usually in the upper income brackets. For more on this topic see "Crisis Point" by New America, February 2020 at https://www.newamerica.org/education-policy/reports/crisis-point-how-enrollment-

management-and-merit-aid-arms-race-are-destroying-public-higher-education/

Associated with reduced funding from state governments for education, there is often insufficient access to affordable health care services for the poor. The pandemic of 2020 amplified this problem as almost 40 million Americans lost their jobs in April and May. While not all jobs lost were lower income ones requiring limited skill levels, for many affected, they also lost their health care insurance or had to begin paying for premiums on their own.

The distribution of expenditures on health care is not as lopsided as education, but the top 10% account for almost 18% of all annual health care expenditures and are greater than the lowest three deciles combined. The implication: those in the upper incomes are more likely to obtain the health care they need, while those with lower incomes are less likely to be able to afford health care services. And this is part of the reason people with higher incomes tend to have longer life spans than people in the lower income quintiles. Keep in mind about 11% of the U.S. population did not have health insurance before the pandemic of 2020. In the midst of the pandemic the share is likely above 20%.

Rationale for the Policy Prescriptions | 43

Health Expenditures by Household Income Decile
Annual Dollars in 2017

Source: Bureau of Labor Statistics, Consumer Expenditure Survey, released September 2018.

The cost of higher education has been increasing about eight [8] time faster than the increase in wages which in part is attributed to states reducing what they are willing to contribute to public institutions – and to cope with lower funding, the universities raise tuition. It is obvious then that those in the top income brackets have better access to both private and increasingly expensive public institutions. Combining the distribution of expenditures on education with health care makes one realize that those in the lower income strata have a lower chance for success than those in the higher income strata. Reducing income inequality is all about advancement or mobility – and in the U.S. there is less opportunity for advancement for those in the lower income quintiles. And, "overall state funding for public two- and four-year colleges in the school year ending in 2018 was more than $7 billion below its 2008 level, after adjusting for inflation." [Center on Budget and Policy Priorities, "State Higher Education Funding Cuts Have Pushed Costs to Students, Worsening Inequality," October 2019 at https://www.cbpp.org/research/state-budget-and-tax/state-higher-education-funding-cuts-have-pushed-costs-to-students.]

It seems as if the American dream is alive and well for those who can afford health care and education. For those that cannot afford these "basics" there are limited opportunities. The focus of this study is on our income tax system and the manner in which it amplifies income inequality.

Linking Income Taxes and Inequality

This section covers three topics – poverty, health and education – all are directly related to the "general welfare" stated in the constitution. This section relates these topics to inequality and describes the manner in which inequality can be reduced, while at the same time increasing our country's productivity.

Poverty

There is a direct link between poverty and the federal program called Social Security. There have been a number of studies that have examined the role of social security related to poverty and the most recent is a report dated February 20, 2020 by the Center on Budget and Policy Priorities. The report states the following:

> "Social Security benefits play a vital role in reducing poverty in every state, and they lift more Americans above the poverty line than any other program. Without Social Security, 21.7 million more Americans would be poor, according to analysis using the March 2019 Current Population Survey. Although most of those whom Social Security keeps out of poverty are elderly, 6.9 million are under age 65, including 1.2

million children. Social Security is particularly important for elderly women and people of color, who have fewer retirement resources outside of Social Security. Depending on their design, reductions in Social Security benefits could significantly increase poverty, particularly among the elderly."

Social Security is funded by the Payroll Tax which is reviewed in detail in a later section of this study. Generally, the Payroll Tax is paid by employees and employers on earned income and is allocated to three major components [1] Social Security, [2] Medicare and [3] Unemployment Insurance.

Social security is composed of two trust funds: The Old-Age and Survivors Insurance (OASI) Trust Fund, which pays retirement and survivors benefits, and the Disability Insurance (DI) Trust Fund. The Payroll Tax – by which employees contribute about 6.2% of their earned income – goes to both of these trust funds with OASI receiving 5.3% and DI receiving 0.9%. What is emphasized is that contributions to Social Security, vis-à-vis the Payroll Tax, only come from earned income – in spite of the fact that a significant portion of a person's income in the higher income quintiles comes from sources other than earned income [carried interest, interest from tax free municipal bonds, ordinary dividends, qualified dividends, long-term capital gain, short term capital gains and ordinary interest].

At the same time, we learn from the April 22, 2020 Trustee report that the Social Security fund will run out of money in 2035. From the report at
https://www.ssa.gov/OACT/TR/2020/tr2020.pdf
the following is taken:

Under the intermediate assumptions, the projected hypothetical combined OASI and DI Trust Fund asset reserves become depleted and unable to pay scheduled benefits in full on a timely basis in 2035.

Under the Trustees' intermediate assumptions, Social Security's total cost is projected to be less than its total income in 2020 and higher than its total income in 2021 and all later years. Social Security's cost has exceeded its non-interest income since 2010.

The reserves of the combined OASI and DI Trust Funds along with projected program income are sufficient to cover projected program cost over the next 10 years under the intermediate assumptions. However, the ratio of reserves to annual cost is projected to decline from 261 percent at the beginning of 2020 to 94 percent at the beginning of 2030. Because this ratio falls below 100 percent by the beginning of the 11th projection year, the combined OASI and DI Trust Funds fail the Trustees' test of short-range financial adequacy.

Basically, the trust funds are slowly running out of money – and yet this program has been shown to lift people out of poverty. The annual report of the Trustees contains many tables and charts showing the funds, the size of the reserves and the decline in assets. The Trustees make the following recommendation:

> Lawmakers have a broad continuum of policy options that would close or reduce Social Security's long-term financing shortfall. Cost estimates for many such policy options are available at www.ssa.gov/OACT/solvency/provisions/. The Trustees recommend that lawmakers address the projected trust fund shortfalls in a timely way in order to phase in necessary changes gradually and give workers and beneficiaries time to adjust to them.

Since inequality is a danger that slowly eats away at the fabric of our society – and retards economic growth – I believe the Social Security trust funds should be maintained. To this end, I offer two solutions to address the upcoming insolvency.

First, all income that is not "earned income" should be subject to payroll taxes. Since the top 1% of all households own about 40% of all the wealth in the U.S. and the top quintile owns over 90% of the wealth, this means most of the payments from non-earned income will be paid by the higher income groups. And, there will be no employer contribution – just the contribution of the asset owner. This contribution will be in addition to the contribution on earned income, and subject to the same rate and income limits as that for earned income.

The 6.2% Payroll Tax will be applied to all non-earned income except monies from retirement accounts [IRA, 401k, 403b], pensions and social security benefits since payroll taxes have already been paid on these sources. The Payroll Tax will only apply to non-earned income greater than $400 per year – the same rule applied to payroll taxes on self-employed individuals. In addition, the 6.2% Payroll Tax will be applied to the first $137,700 of non-earned income for 2020 – which is the same rate and income limit for earned income. This recommendation will increase the income and assets in the trust fund. Non-earned income includes Special Income [Long-Term Capital Gains, Carried Interest, Qualified Dividends and the interest from Tax Free Municipal Bonds] plus ordinary interest, ordinary dividends and short-term capital gains]. Thus, non-earned income is larger than the Special Income category detailed in this study.

Second, based on longer lifespans, it is recommended that the age for full retirement be increased two years for those born after 1990. This will have the effect of delaying the outflow of funds for younger generations.

The combination of these two recommendations will delay the insolvency of the trust funds by years.

Health

There are two broad categories discussed in this section – Medicare and Medicaid. Medicare Part A [hospital portion] is funded by the Payroll Tax while Medicaid [at the Federal level] is funded through general revenue. There is no dedicated source of revenue for Medicaid.

If everyone in the United States were healthy, our country would have fewer sick days used by employees and the working population would be more productive – which would lead to a more robust economy. Concurrent with this, there would be less stress on the health care system and the health sector would be a smaller share of Gross Domestic Product or GDP. In keeping with the constitution, everyone in the United States should have access to affordable health care. This is critical for individuals to be productive members of society.

The Affordable Care Act [ACA] was a comprehensive health care law enacted in March 2010. The main goals of the ACA were the following:

- To make affordable healthcare available to more people
- To expand the Medicaid program

- To Support techniques to lower health care costs

Much has been written and debated about this act, but it did have the impact of increasing the number of people with health insurance. And – under the ACA – insurance companies were not allowed to discriminate based on a person's pre-existing medical conditions.

Estimates from the U.S. Congressional Budget Office or CBO reveal there were an estimated 47 million people in the U.S., or 16% of the population, **without** health insurance in 2010 before the ACA was enacted. In 2016 this number of people without health insurance had declined to 27 million people or 9% of the population. Since Mr. Trump became President, the number of people without health insurance has increased to 30.1 million or 11.1% of the population in 2018.

The President has endorsed the repeal of the ACA and the President and the Republican party now have lawsuits before the Supreme Court to repeal key components of the ACA. In addition, the U.S. Congressional Budget Office revised and increased the number of people without health insurance in their May 2019 report compared to their forecast of uninsured people from 2016. The new forecast takes into account current administration policies and the number of uninsured people rises to 40 million or 13% of the population in 2026. The CBO's earlier estimate from 2016 was that there would be 28 million uninsured or 10% of the population in 2026.

What about the 40 million people that lost their jobs in the 2020 pandemic? If 20 million of the 40 million people that lost their job also lost their health insurance, and each of those persons that lost their job and health insurance had a family that used the employer sponsored health insurance, it is not unreasonable to think an additional 50 million people in the U.S. might not have health insurance. This would more than double the number of uninsured Americans to more than 80 million people or 24% of the U.S. population. This may be the issue of our time.

No alternative health bill is under review or discussion, and the current administration's focus is to reduce Medicaid by providing states with block grants.

In other words, the current administration does not view health care as a priority.

The pandemic in the Spring of 2020 resulted in the enactment of the "Coronavirus Aid, Relief, and Economic Security Act" or the "CARES Act" in March 2020. While the CARES Act provides resources to hospitals and private companies to help cover COVID19-related costs, it does not expand health coverage, and with almost 40 million people losing their jobs in April and May 2020, it is possible that more than 80 million people in the U.S. do not have health insurance.

The CARES Act allocated about $150 billion to state and local governments – which is less than half of the $350 billion allocated to small business. And State and local governments help treat pandemic victims.

During the campaign period for the 2020 democratic primaries – before the pandemic was even on the radar screen – there was a lot of discussion on health care with some candidates promoting some form of universal health care. I do not endorse universal health care, but I do think we – as a country – need to make sure everyone has access to affordable health care.

To this end I support the continuation of Medicare and Medicaid and will discuss some of the important points about these programs before providing my recommendations.

Linking Income Taxes and Inequality

Medicare

Medicare funding comes from the Payroll Tax and according to the report summary of the April 22, 2020 Trustee report, see https://www.cms.gov/files/document/2020-medicare-trustees-report.pdf, we learn the following:

> The Medicare program helps pay for health care services for the aged, disabled, and individuals with end-stage renal disease. It has two separate trust funds, the Hospital Insurance (HI) Trust Fund and the Supplementary Medical Insurance (SMI) Trust Fund. HI, otherwise known as Medicare Part A, helps pay for inpatient hospital services, skilled nursing facility and home health services following hospital stays, and hospice care. The SMI Trust Fund consists of separate accounts for Medicare Part B and Part D. Part B helps pay for physician, outpatient hospital, home health, and other services for individuals who have voluntarily enrolled. Part D provides subsidized access to drug insurance coverage on a voluntary basis for all beneficiaries, as well as premium and cost-sharing subsidies for low-income enrollees.

> The projections and analysis in this report do not reflect the potential effects of the COVID-19 pandemic on the Medicare program. Given the uncertainty associated with these impacts, the trustees believe that it is not possible to adjust the estimates accurately at this time.
>
> The estimated depletion date for the HI trust fund is 2026, the same as in last year's report. As in past years, the Trustees have determined that the fund is not adequately financed over the next 10 years. HI income is projected to be lower than last year's estimates due to lower payroll taxes.

The results of the report are grim as the Medicare financial reserves will be depleted by 2026. That is right around the corner.

To increase the funding for Medicare, I suggest a program similar to that proposed in the Social Security section – that the Payroll Tax be applied to all Unearned Income – LTCG, qualified dividends, Carried Interest, interest from Tax-Free Municipal bonds, regular interest, ordinary dividends and short-term capital gains. For Medicare, the payroll tax for the asset holders of wealth would be 1.45% and there would be no income limits – which differs from the Social Security payroll Tax – and there would be no employer contribution. Payroll taxes on Medicare would begin when non-earned income is greater than $400 per year – the same rule that applies to earned income of self-employed individuals. With about $1 trillion of Special Income in 2015, this would have totaled more than $14.5 billion in revenue for Medicare that year – just from Special Income. The other categories of non-earned income [ordinary dividends, ordinary interest and short-term capital gains] would provide additional revenue. The lack of income limits in this recommendation is consistent with the Medicare Payroll Tax currently in place.

The government has already implemented a tax along these lines called "The Net Investment Income Tax" or NIIT that gets activated when adjusted gross income exceeds a certain level. It adds an additional 2.35% to the existing Payroll Tax amount of 1.45%. This tax is only levied on investment income and I delve into this later in the Payroll Tax Basics section of this study.

Medicaid

Medicaid is the U.S.'s health insurance program for low income individuals and covers about 20% of the population – which is the lowest income quintiles or 25 million households in 2015. There is no dedicated source of funding for Medicaid.

Medicaid is organized as a partnership between the U.S. federal government and state governments. The Medicaid entitlement program is based on two pillars:

- All persons meeting the income eligibility requirements per a specified formula will receive health coverage.
- The Federal government will match the state expenditures on Medicaid for those that qualify for the program.

The program was enacted in 1972 and has changed over time. The chart below plots these changes and comes from the Kaiser Foundation website at https://www.kff.org/medicaid/issue-brief/10-things-to-know-about-medicaid-setting-the-facts-straight/?gclid=EAIaIQobChMI6I6jzPyy6AIVr4VaBR1M5Ai8EAAYASAAEgIPBPD_BwE

Medicaid Has Evolved Over Time

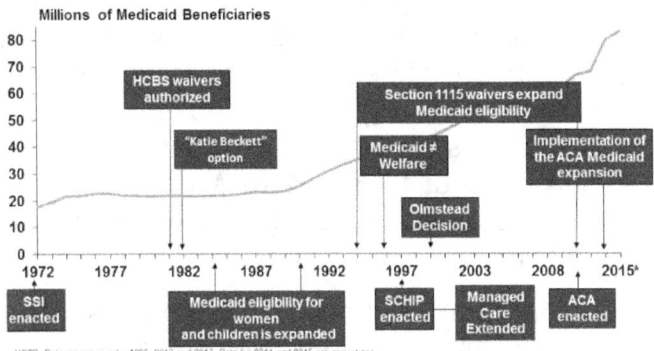

An important date to note in the chart was 2010 when the ACA was enacted that allowed expansion of Medicaid. Since 2010, 35 states have expanded Medicaid under the ACA [see https://www.healthinsurance.org/medicaid/].

Since there are no dedicated sources of funding for the Federal program, funding for Medicaid comes from the general fund and is subject to Congressional debate every year.

In 2017, Medicaid spending totaled about $592 billion and the Federal portion of that was about $370 billion or 62% of the total.

My first recommendation is that Medicaid have a dedicated source of funding and that it be similar to Medicare. My second recommendation is that the dedicated source of funding be a payroll tax of 1.45% on all non-earned income [which includes Special Income plus ordinary interest, ordinary dividends and short-term capital gains] with no income limits. For 2015 this would have been more than $14.5 billion or about 4% of federal Medicaid expenditures in that year [which were about $348 billion.]

In addition, my third recommendation is that funding for Medicaid receive 1.5% of individual income taxes. Recall from the Personal Income Tax section earlier that I recommended that the top income tax bracket be raised to 40% from 37% and all income categories be subject to the same tax. I am suggesting that one half of that increase, or 1.5% of that additional revenue, be dedicated to the Medicaid program.

Linking Income Taxes and Inequality | 63

Education

Possessing skills that are needed in the labor market is key to working and being productive. The primary programs of the U.S. Federal government related to post-secondary education are grants and loans. Grant programs provide funding for individuals to receive degree program coursework, specific skill training, as well as funding for research projects. As we have already learned, a larger portion of aid is being allocated to wealthier students who do not need the aid.

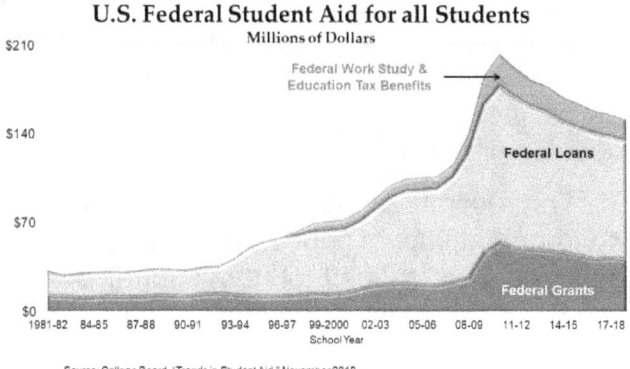

Source: College Board. "Trends in Student Aid," November 2019.

Total student aid from the federal government peaked in school year 2010-11 at about $201 million and has declined about $52 million or 25% to $151 million in 2018-19.

Interestingly, the state governments are the primary source of funding for post-secondary education. With the 2008 recession, state spending on post-secondary education fell with the burden being passed to students in the form of higher tuition. As has already been shown, those in the higher income brackets can afford to pay the increased tuition and spend a disproportionate amount of total household spending on education. Those in the lower quintiles do not have the resources for skill advancement.

What is needed is for the Federal government to begin providing funding to post-secondary educational institutions to insure those in the lowest income quintiles can get training and develop or enhance skills.

My first recommendation is that the Federal government supplement state funding of post-secondary education [not grants for students, but payments to the educational institutions]. In conjunction with the additional federal funding, states would have to allow students to attend trade schools or the first two years of college using the means-tested approach already adopted by Medicaid *if the students meet the academic requirements*. So, if someone qualifies for Medicaid, they automatically qualify for free additional training at trade schools or the first two years of college. And, if someone qualifies for free training at trade schools or the first two years of college, they automatically qualify for Medicaid. Remember, Medicaid is the program that provides health insurance to the lowest household income quintiles.

Part of the funding for the program can come from personal income tax, and part can come from an additional payroll tax. Just as a reminder, this study is focusing on inequality so I am recommending that those with the highest incomes fund the education component. Here is my vision of how it would work.

- **Payroll Tax** – There are two recommendations here. First is that the federal education program institute a dedicated source of funding from the payroll tax. Second, a Payroll Tax of 2% be applied to all non-earned Income. There would be no limit on income – similar to what I have recommended for Medicare and Medicaid. This payroll tax would only be applied to non-earned income greater than $400 per year. For 2015 this 2% tax on non-earned income would translate to about $20 billion [Recall Special Income totaled about $1 trillion in 2015 and non-earned income is greater than Special Income.] There would be no employer contribution, just the contribution from the owner of the assets that generated the income.

- **Personal Income Taxes** – I've already recommended that the top income tax bracket be raised to 40% from 37% and that all income categories be subject to the same tax. Thus, one half of that increase, or 1.5%, of the additional revenue should be dedicated to this educational component.

Personal Income Tax Basics

A personal income tax is a tax imposed by the government on an individual or family. Personal income taxes in the United States are based on the premise that people earning more income can afford to pay more taxes. This is called a progressive tax system and the chart below shows the brackets and tax rates for the U.S. federal government's personal income taxes for 2015 for four categories of tax filers:
- Single Individuals
- Married Couples Filing Jointly
- Married Couples Filing Separately
- Head of Households

2015 Tax Rate Schedules

Single	
Tax Rate	Taxable Income
10.0%	$0 to $9,225
15.0%	$9,225 to $37,450
25.0%	$37,450 to $90,750
28.0%	$90,750 to $189,300
33.0%	$189,300 to $411,500
35.0%	$411,500 to $413,200
39.6%	$413,200+

Married Filing Jointly	
Tax Rate	Taxable Income
10.0%	$0 to $18,450
15.0%	$18,450 to $74,900
25.0%	$74,900 to $151,200
28.0%	$151,200 to $230,450
33.0%	$230,450 to $411,500
35.0%	$411,500 to $464,850
39.6%	$464,850+

Head of Household	
Tax Rate	Taxable Income
10.0%	$0 to $13,150
15.0%	$13,150 to $50,200
25.0%	$50,200 to $129,600
28.0%	$129,600 to $209,850
33.0%	$209,850 to $411,500
35.0%	$411,500 to $439,000
39.6%	$439,000+

Married Filing Separately	
Tax Rate	Taxable Income
10.0%	$0 to $9,225
15.0%	$9,225 to $37,450
25.0%	$37,450 to $75,600
28.0%	$75,600 to $115,225
33.0%	$115,225 to $205,750
35.0%	$205,750 to $232,450
39.6%	$232,425+

Each category has the same tax rates. What varies is the income level and income brackets to which the rate is applied. For example, in the single taxpayer category, the lowest bracket is under $9,225 and is 10%. The next bracket goes from $9,225 to $37,450 and is 15%. For the married taxpayer filing jointly, the lowest bracket is under $18,450 and is 10%. The next bracket goes from $18,450 to $74,900 and is 15%.

The Process for Computing Tax Liability

Once a year, each individual files an annual income tax return with the U.S. Internal Revenue Service. The individual gets forms from their employer and financial institutions that specifies income for the previous year. Income is from all categories and includes earned income from employment, interest earned, dividends earned, capital gains, carried interest, self-employment income, pensions and social security benefits. Each of these categories is part of an individual's total income.

The forms providing this key tax information typically arrive between the third week of January and the third week of February and are documents for the previous year that are needed to prepare one's tax return. It is typical to make payments throughout the year so one's tax liability is paid over time – and not a lump sum payment when the forms are due April 15th. If you make quarterly payments to the IRS, the 4th quarterly payment for the previous year's income is due January 15th – weeks before all income documents will be received. This means taxpayers have to "guess" what their total income will be for the entire year.

The household-taxpayer needs to compile the information on the documents he/she receives

70 | Personal Income Tax Basics

on forms created by the IRS and submit the forms to the IRS by April 15. One can download the forms from the IRS website or have the IRS mail them to your household. The forms can be submitted on paper, or they can be filed electronically.

In 2015 the basic method for computing one's tax liability was to add all of your income sources together. This is not as simple as it may seem since several of the income categories differ from the other categories [social security benefits that are counted as taxable income are based on a formula that is difficult to compute]. After total income is computed there are reductions to the total based on an amount deemed necessary to live. This is called the "standard deduction." If a taxpayer desires, they can outline their own deductions and submit "itemized deductions" in lieu of the standard deduction. In 2015 taxpayers also got an allowance for the number of people in the household and this was called the "personal exemption." Subtracting the standard deduction and the personal exemptions from adjusted gross income leave you with taxable income. Once you have taxable income, it is a simple matter of using the tax tables the IRS provides. For those with more complex computations – those that have Special Income – there are preferential tax rates that make the computations more complex – but reduce tax liability.

Further, if your tax return has certain characteristics, you may be subject to the Alternative Minimum Tax or AMT, which means you have to compute your tax liability a second time using a different methodology to determine your tax bill.

Under the "Tax Cuts and Jobs Act of 2017" some of this changed. Personal exemptions were excluded and the standard deduction was increased. For people with certain types of income, their taxable income was reduced by 20% due to the "Pass Through" provision that affected part of their income under the Act.

Removing personal exemptions made the computations simpler, but adding the Pass-Through provision made the computations more complex.

My recommendations for personal income taxes are straightforward.

- Have all categories of income taxed at the same tax rate. There would be no preferential tax rates for LTCG, carried interest, qualified dividends or interest from tax-free municipal bonds.

- Increase the standard deduction by 50%.
- Eliminate itemized deductions.
- Remove the 20% Pass through from business
- Raise the highest income tax bracket to 40%

Administratively, I recommend the following:

- Have all income paid to the taxpayer be recorded using the cash method. This primarily applies to Special Income categories where some of the data are based on the accrual method.
- Have all tax documents reporting income sent to the individuals by the third week of January.
- Have the 4th quarterly payment due the middle of February – after one receives their tax documents.

Computing Long-Term Capital Gains [LTCG] Taxes

How does the LTCG tax rate work? And, how does one qualify to use the LTCG tax rate?

The U.S. Treasury Department, Internal Revenue Service (IRS) provides details on computing capital gains at https://www.irs.gov/taxtopics/tc409. The information below is from the IRS web site.

> When a person sells an asset, the sale normally results in a capital gain or loss. There are several examples of assets people sell that can result in a gain or loss. These include:
> - Property – including homes – that someone inherits
> - Property that someone owns for personal use or as an investment
> - Cars
> - Investments, such as stocks and bonds

Determining a Gain or Loss

To determine a capital gain or loss on an asset, sellers must compute the difference between the basis, usually what they paid for the property, and what they received for it. Capital gains and losses are either long or short term, depending on how long the taxpayer holds the property. The gain or loss is short-term for taxpayers who hold it for one year or less.

Capital Losses

Taxpayers whose capital losses are more than their capital gains can deduct the difference as losses on their tax returns, up to $3,000 per year, or $1,500 if married and filing a separate return. When their total net capital loss is more than the limit they can deduct, taxpayers can carry it over to next year's tax return.

Capital loss deductions are applicable to the sale of investment property, but not on the sale of property held for personal use.

> **Capital Gains**
>
> For Taxpayers whose long-term gains are more than their long-term losses, the difference between the two is a net long-term capital gain. If the net long-term capital gain is more than the net short-term capital loss, it's a net capital gain.
>
> The tax rate on a net capital gain usually depends on income. The maximum tax rate on a net capital gain is 20%, but for most taxpayers a zero percent or 15% rate will apply. In addition, capital gains may be subject to the net investment income tax of 3.8% when income is above certain amounts.

The IRS has a special form to compute capital gains and it is Schedule D. This form divides capital gains into short-run gains – which are taxed at your marginal tax rate, and LTCG that are taxed at the preferential rates.

Personal residences are subject to an exclusion of capital gains taxes up to $500,000 for a married couple filing jointly. There are many ins and outs, but there are definite benefits to holding an asset longer than one year – which means it qualifies as a LTCG. In addition, a special category of dividend – "Qualified Dividends" – is subject to the same tax rate as LTCG.

What are these qualified dividends?

They are dividends that meet specific criteria to be taxed at the lower LTCG tax rate rather than at higher tax rate for an individual's ordinary income. The rates on qualified dividends range from 0 to 20%, and, if your modified adjusted gross income is greater than $250,000, the Net Investment Income Tax of 3.8% is also applied.

Another category of income that receives preferential tax treatment is "Carried Interest" which is classified in the tax code as a capital gain. Carried interest is a share of the profits [20% to 25%] that the general partners of a private equity or hedge fund receive as compensation. The tax rate on carried interest is the same as that of LTCG.

The rate of taxation on LTCG, Qualified Dividends and Carried Interest is a function of income level and filing status [single, married filing jointly, married filing separately or head of

Personal Income Tax Basics | 77

household]. Shown below are the LTCG tax rates for all four filing categories.

Long Term Capital Gains 2015 Tax Rates

Single	
Tax Rate	Taxable Income
0.0%	$0 to $9,225
0.0%	$9,225 to $37,450
15.0%	$37,450 to $90,750
15.0%	$90,750 to $189,300
15.0%	$189,300 to $411,500
15.0%	$411,500 to $413,200
20.0%	$413,200+

Married Filing Jointly	
Tax Rate	Taxable Income
0.0%	$0 to $18,450
0.0%	$18,450 to $74,900
15.0%	$74,900 to $151,200
15.0%	$151,200 to $230,450
15.0%	$230,450 to $411,500
15.0%	$411,500 to $464,850
20.0%	$464,850+

Head of Household	
Tax Rate	Taxable Income
0.0%	$0 to $13,150
0.0%	$13,150 to $50,200
15.0%	$50,200 to $129,600
15.0%	$129,600 to $209,850
15.0%	$209,850 to $411,500
15.0%	$411,500 to $439,000
20.0%	$439,000+

Married Filing Separately	
Tax Rate	Taxable Income
0.0%	$0 to $9,225
0.0%	$9,225 to $37,450
15.0%	$37,450 to $75,600
15.0%	$75,600 to $115,225
15.0%	$115,225 to $205,750
15.0%	$205,750 to $232,450
20.0%	$232,425+

Two key points:

- The income brackets match those of the regular tax brackets
- The LTCG tax rates are either 0%, 15% or 20%.

You can see for a married couple filing a joint return, the LTCG tax rate for income above $464,850 is 20% – almost half of the tax rate for regular income in the same bracket. This is the preferential tax rate. And if we compare the

78 | Personal Income Tax Basics

LTCG tax rate with that of the lowest income tax bracket, we see it is nearer the lower bracket than the upper bracket.

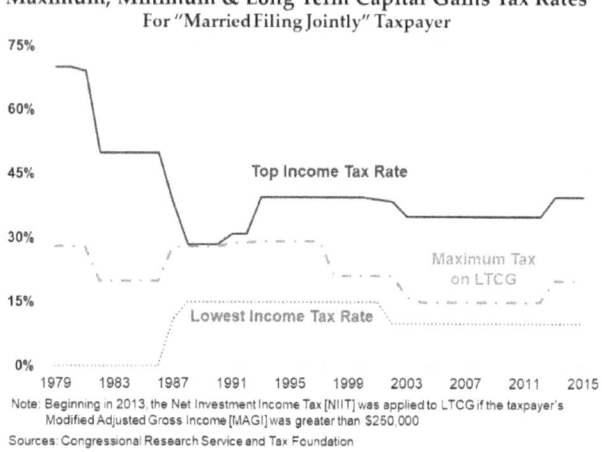

Since 2000, the difference between the maximum LTCG tax and the maximum individual income tax rate has averaged about 19%. That is to say, the LTCG tax is about 19% lower than the individual income tax rate for the highest bracket. By contrast, the maximum LTCG tax rate is only 7.5% higher than the lowest individual income tax rate. Taxpayers in the upper income strata have a very good deal with LTCG tax rates.

The last category of income reviewed is interest from Tax Exempt Municipal Bonds. The interest received from these tax-free bonds is not subject to federal income taxes under the federal laws. In most states, the interest income from these municipal bonds is also tax free if the municipality issuing the bonds is within the state.

So those are the categories of income that have preferential income tax rates when compared to the individual income tax brackets specified under the U.S. tax law.

My recommendations for Special Income:

- Eliminate preferential tax rates for LTCG, Qualified Dividends, Carried Interest and interest from Tax Fee Municipal Bonds

- Use the tax rates in the tax schedule for all non-earned income – which includes Special Income categories. Thus, there are no preferential tax rates, no complex computations and all income is taxed the same.

Computing the Alternative Minimum Tax [AMT]

The Alternative Minimum Tax is complex. For taxpayers, you compute your income taxes two times and pay the higher amount from each of the two calculations. The IRS devotes a web page to this topic at https://www.irs.gov/taxtopics/tc556 and the information below is from that website.

> Under the tax law, certain tax benefits can significantly reduce a taxpayer's regular tax amount. The alternative minimum tax (AMT) applies to taxpayers with high economic income by setting a limit on those benefits. It helps to ensure that those taxpayers pay at least a minimum amount of tax.

How Is the AMT Calculated?

The AMT is the excess of the tentative minimum tax over the regular tax. Thus, the AMT is owed only if the tentative minimum tax for the year is greater than the regular tax for that year. The tentative minimum tax is figured separately from the regular tax. In general, compute the tentative minimum tax by:

1. Computing taxable income eliminating or reducing certain exclusions and deductions, and taking into account differences with respect to when certain items are taken into account in computing regular taxable income and alternative minimum taxable income (AMTI),
2. Subtracting the AMT exemption amount,
3. Multiplying the amount computed in (2) by the appropriate AMT tax rates, and
4. Subtracting the AMT foreign tax credit.

The law sets the AMT exemption amounts and AMT tax rates. Taxpayers can use the special capital gain rates in effect for the regular tax if they're lower than the AMT tax rates that would otherwise apply. In addition, some tax credits that reduce regular tax liability don't reduce AMT tax liability.

Am I Subject to the AMT?
To find out if you may be subject to the AMT, refer to the **Alternative Minimum Tax (AMT)** line instructions in the Instructions for Form 1040 and 1040-SR (PDF). If subject to the AMT, you may be required to complete and attach Form 6251, Alternative Minimum Tax – Individuals. See the Instructions for Form 6251.

Am I Eligible for a Tax Credit?
If you're not liable for AMT this year, but you paid AMT in one or more previous years, you may be eligible to take a special minimum tax credit against your regular tax this year.

There are two attributes about this test from the IRS that are noteworthy. First, undertaking the computations is cumbersome. And second, taxpayers are allowed to apply LTCG tax rates to their income even if AMT computations imply a higher tax rate. In other words, the AMT does not remove preferential tax rates for LTCG, Qualified Dividends or Carried Interest. And, most of the wealth that leads to income from these categories resides in the top income quintile.

Under the Tax Cuts and Jobs Act of 2017, the exemption under the AMT was increased significantly. While individuals and corporations had to undertake the computations in 2015, the AMT is not in use very much in 2020 due to changes from the Tax Act of 2017 and the IRS provides limited support for this topic on their website.

My recommendation is to eliminate the AMT altogether.

The Tax Cuts and Jobs Act of 2017

The Tax Cuts and Jobs Act of 2017 was signed into law by President Trump on December 22, 2017 and was the largest tax overhaul since 1986. The law made some significant changes to the tax codes for individuals and businesses. The following discussion highlights the changes for each of the two categories.

Individuals

- Lowered the tax rates for all but two of the brackets [the lowest remained at 10% and the second highest at 35%]. The new tax brackets and tax rates for each class of filer is shown below.

2019 Tax Rate Schedule Under the 2017 Tax Act

Single	
Tax Rate	Taxable Income
10.0%	Up to $9,700
12.0%	$9,701 to $39,475
22.0%	$39,476 to $84,200
24.0%	$84,201 to $160,725
32.0%	$160,726 to $204,100
35.0%	$204,101 to $510,300
37.0%	Over $510,300

Married Filing Jointly	
Tax Rate	Taxable Income
10.0%	Up to $19,400
12.0%	$19,401 to $78,950
22.0%	$78,951 to $168,400
24.0%	$168,401 to $321,450
32.0%	$321,451 to $408,200
35.0%	$408,201 to $612,350
37.0%	Over $612,350

Head of Household	
Tax Rate	Taxable Income
10.0%	Up to $13,850
12.0%	$13,851 to $52,850
22.0%	$52,851 to $84,200
24.0%	$84,201 to $160,700
32.0%	$160,701 to $204,100
35.0%	$204,101 to $510,300
37.0%	Over $510,300

Married Filing Separately	
Tax Rate	Taxable Income
10.0%	Up to $9,700
12.0%	$9,701 to $39,475
22.0%	$39,476 to $84,200
24.0%	$84,201 to $160,725
32.0%	$160,726 to $204,100
35.0%	$204,101 to $306,175
37.0%	Over $306,175

- Eliminated Personal Exemptions
- Expanded the Standard Deduction
    - Single increased to $12,200 from $6,500 in 2017.
    - Married Filing Jointly increased to $24,000 from $13,000 in 2017.
    - Married Filing Separately increased to $12,200 from $6,500 in 2017.
    - Head of Household increased to $18,350 from $9,550 in 2017.
- For itemized deductions, put restrictions on the amount that could be deducted for mortgage interest paid and state and local taxes paid.
- Doubled the child tax credit to $2,000 with up to $1,400 being refundable.
- Reformed the Alternative Minimum Tax by increasing the exemptions from $84,500 to $109,400 for a married couple filing jointly and by increasing the phaseout of the exemption from $160,900 to $1 million.
- All of the individual taxes end in 2025 and the system reverts to the system in place in 2017 – before the Tax Act of 2017 was passed.

Details of the Tax Act can be viewed in IRS publication 5307: "Tax Reform: Basics for Individuals and Families" and at https://www.irs.gov/newsroom/publication-5307-tax-reform-basics-for-individuals-and-families

Businesses

- Section 199a – a new provision that allows a deduction of 20% for qualified business income, including real estate investment trusts – to be passed on to individuals. While this does not alter business income tax liability, it reduces the personal income tax liability of the individual receiving the income.
- The top corporate tax rate is reduced to 21% from 35%.
- The deduction for interest is limited to 30% of adjusted taxable income for firms with a debt to equity ratio greater than 1.5. Interest above that can be carried forward indefinitely.
- Payments for lobbying to local councils are allowed.
- Non-corporate taxpayers may be subject to excess business loss limitations.

- For most taxpayers, there is no longer the option to carry a loss to a previous year – losses can only be carried forward.
- There are changes to rules for like-kind exchanges.
- No deductions are allowed for payments made in sexual harassment cases.
- There is 100% expensing of capital investments. This is phased out over 5 years.

There are too many changes to review all in detail here. To view the complete list of changes of the Tax Act, see IRS publication 5318: "Tax Reform: What's New for Your Business" and at
https://www.irs.gov/newsroom/tax-cuts-and-jobs-act-a-comparison-for-businesses

Results from the Tax Act

Three categories of results are reviewed from the Tax Act of 2017 – the economic effects, the effects on U.S. Debt, and the distributional effect.

- **Economic Effects of the Tax Act of 2017** – According to the U.S. Congressional Budget Office [see "CBO Confirms GOP Tax Law Contributes to Darkening Fiscal Future," February 5, 2019] "The tax law boosted the economy last year … Beyond this temporary boost, the tax law does not change our longer-term path of growth … there is no evidence that it is making a meaningful difference for families that are struggling financially …"

- **Effects of the Tax Act of 2017 on U.S. Debt** – According to the U.S. CBO, February, 2019 "CBO projected that the tax cut will add $1.9 trillion to deficits over 10 years …" The Director of the CBO stated: "the economy isn't likely to grow quickly enough to shrink the budget deficit."

- **Distributional Effect of the Tax Act of 2017** – According to the Tax Policy Center ["Effects of the Tax Cuts and

Jobs Act: A Preliminary Analysis," June 2018] "After-tax income will increase by a greater percentage for high-income than for low-income households. The boost in after-tax income is 0.4 percent for households in the lowest quintile, compared with 2.9 percent for those in the top quintile, more than 4 percent for those in the 95th–99th percentile, and 3.4 percent for taxpayers in the top 1 percent." ... "Diving deeper, the distribution of the pass-through provisions in the TCJA are even more regressive. According to JCT (2018), 44 percent of the benefit of the pass-through provision in 2018 will accrue to households earning more than $1,000,000 per year. Only 2 percent of the benefit will accrue to households making $50,000 or less."

These findings are disconcerting and highlight the fact that the Tax Cuts and Jobs Bill of 2017 adds more debt to the country's debt burden, does not stimulate economic growth and primarily benefits the wealthy. It amplifies inequality and does little to help those in the lowest quintiles.

Recommendations

- Eliminate the 20% pass-through provision [Section 199a] which is a business tax, but has ramifications for individual taxes.
- Eliminate the Alternative Minimum Tax.
- Eliminate all deductions for depreciation.
- Make capital expenditures deductible in the year they are made.
- Eliminate all interest expense deductions.
- Eliminate all deductions for expenses for all lobbying.
- Only allow loss-carry forward for one year into the future.
- Leave the top corporate tax rate at 21%.

Under Reporting Income

Not everyone reports all their income – and the IRS estimates the difference between tax liability and taxes actually paid. This difference is called the "Tax Gap" and for 2016, the IRS estimates the gap was $408 billion or 18% of federal tax liability. According to the IRS, the largest portion of the Tax Gap [$125 billion or 30% of the gap] comes from business income that goes to owners of the companies such as partnerships, S Corporations and sole proprietorships. This underreporting has varied between 19% and 63% for the years 2008 to 2010 and part of the reason people have not been reporting is a lack of enforcement – see https://www.irs.gov/newsroom/the-tax-gap.

Congress has reduced funding for the IRS during the last decade and the IRS staff has been reduced by 14% since 2012. According to CNBC, the chances of an audit fell from 1 in 5 to 1 in 10 and the collections from enforcement are about 10% of the Tax Gap. Those that are benefiting from underreporting are most likely those with the bigger incomes.

My recommendation related to under reporting:

Bring the audit staff of the IRS up to a level that can enforce the tax laws and reduce the tax gap.

Personal Income Tax Basics | 93

Payroll Tax Basics

Payroll taxes are levied to pay for Social Security, Part A of Medicare [the hospital insurance portion] and the federal unemployment insurance program.

Payroll taxes are taxes paid on the wages and salaries earned by employees. Payroll taxes fall into two categories: deductions from an employee's wages, and taxes paid by the employer based on the employee's wages. The employer withholds the money from the employee's pay, and submits it to the government on behalf of the employee. In the United States, the revenue from these taxes pay for Medicare and Social Security and fall under the "Federal Insurance Contributions Act" or FICA. Since 2015 the social security taxes are 12.4% while the Medicare tax is 2.9% for a total of 15.3%. Employees and the employer each pay one-half of the 15.3% or 7.65%.

Over time, the tax rate and income limit have increased from a 1979 level of 6.13% for social security and Medicare. Initially, the upper income limit was established by statute. Since the early 1980s, the adjustment is done automatically based on an inflation adjustment methodology called the cost of living adjustment

[COLA] which is based on the average wage index.

Combined OASDI & Medicare Tax Rates for Employees

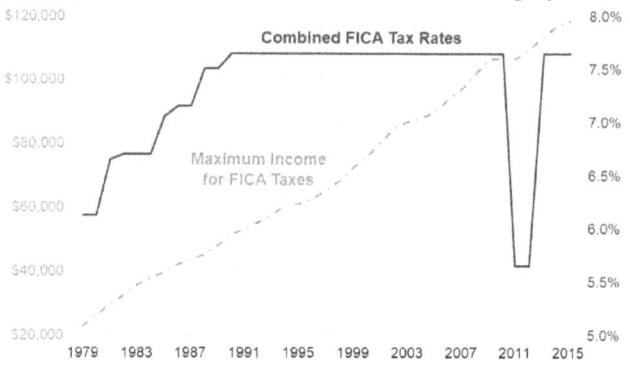

Note. From 1979 to 1990 there was one tax for both OASDI & Medicare.
Beginning in 1991: separate rates for Medicare and OASDI with the Medicare income limit at $125,000
Beginning in 1994 there was no income limit on Medicare taxes
Beginning in 2013 there was an additional 0.9% Medicare tax on incomes above $200,000
In 2011 & 2012 the OASDI rate was cut to 4.2% for employees. The employer rate remained at 6.2%.

Social security taxes are not paid on all income earned and the upper limits have changed over time based on the COLA. In 1979 the income limit was $22,900 which means social security taxes were only paid on the first $22,900 of earned income. This upper limit has increased each year and was $118,500 in 2015 and $137,700 for 2020.

For self-employed individuals, the individual pays both the employee and employer contribution. Also, payroll taxes are due on self-employed income when it is greater than $400 for a calendar year.

The income limits on Medicare taxes are different from social security and it is more complicated to compute. Beginning in 1994, there is no upper income limit on which the Medicare taxes are paid. Beginning in 2013, Medicare payment calculation became more complex with the passage of the Affordable Care Act. If the employee earns more than $200,000 a year in adjusted gross income [the dollar value depends on the taxpayer filing category], the employee and employer each pay an additional 0.9% for a total of 1.45%. And, if the taxpayer has investment income greater than $250,000 [depending on filing category], an additional 3.8% is collected for Medicare under the Net Investment Income Tax [NIIT]. The NIIT level is $250,000 of adjusted gross income for households classified as married filing jointly.

> The NIIT applies at a rate of 3.8% to certain net investment income of individuals, estates and trusts that have income above the statutory threshold amounts.

According to the IRS:

Adjusted Gross Income Limits for the NIIT to activate:

- Single = $200,000
- Married Filing Jointly = $250,000
- Married Filing Separately = $125,000
- Head of Household = $200,000
- Qualifying Widower with Dependent Child = $250,000

As you can tell, computing social security taxes is fairly straightforward, while computing Medicare taxes is a bit more complex.

In the United States, the social security system had its roots in the depression when many people were in poverty and the unemployment rate reached 25%. The program was signed into law by President Roosevelt in 1935 and was designed to help workers after they retired. The social security system has been very successful in reducing elder poverty. In September 2018, a Peterson Foundation publication revealed that elder poverty was 66% before social security, and 16% after social security.

Medicare was started 30 years after social security in 1965 when retirees found it almost impossible to get health insurance after they left employment. Medicare was signed into law by

President Johnson and is now a universal right for Americans after they reach 65.

With regard to payroll taxes, the top quintile has the lowest FICA rates paid as share of income. The reasons are based on the fact that the households in the top quintile have the following:

- Earned incomes above the Social Security Limit
- Non-earned income such as LTCG, carried interest, qualified dividends and interest from tax-free municipal bonds that are not subject to FICA taxes.

Between 1979 and 2005, as FICA tax rates increased and the income level was raised, the lowest quintile share of income that goes to FICA taxes increased – and is now the highest rate of the five quintiles. The FICA tax is regressive as the group with the highest income has the lowest tax rate, and the group with the lowest income has the highest tax rate.

Personal Income Tax Basics

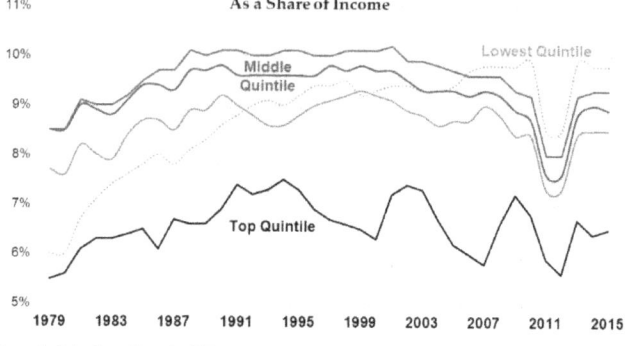

Household FICA Taxes Paid by Quintile
As a Share of Income

Source: Tax Policy Center, December 2018

Keep in mind that these tax rates represent the taxes paid by households – this is the employee contribution. For self-employed individuals, they pay the employee and employer contribution. Whereas the federal tax system is a progressive system, the FICA taxes are regressive.

One recommendation for payroll taxes:

Apply the payroll tax to non-earned Income – which includes Special Income, ordinary dividends, ordinary interest and short-term capital gains. All the rules that apply to payroll taxes on Earned Income should apply to non-earned Income. Payroll taxes would be due on non-earned income greater than $400 in a calendar year.

Business Taxes and Inequality

The focus of this section is on the large corporations in the U.S. There are many types of businesses like Partnerships, self-employed individuals and small companies such as "S Corporations." The variations are many and rather than focus on all type of business entities, the focus is on large corporations.

Regarding paying taxes, companies need to address income taxes, excise taxes and payroll taxes. Company payroll taxes have already been covered in the section titled Payroll Tax Basics, thus, this section focuses on corporate income tax.

The corporation has to have a tax identification number and specify a 12-month period for their reporting year. This can be the calendar year or their fiscal year and the company has to specify the accounting method used – cash or accrual.

The basic concept on corporate income taxation is that the income tax is based on the company's net income. Net income is gross income minus costs – where costs are allowed if they are considered "ordinary and necessary" for the operation of the company. The Internal Revenue Service or IRS produces Publication

535 which reviews business expenses. The

> An ordinary expense is one that is common and accepted in your industry. A necessary expense is one that is helpful and appropriate for your trade or business. An expense does not have to be indispensable to be considered necessary.
>
> Even though an expense may be ordinary and necessary, you may not be allowed to deduct the expense in the year you paid or incurred it. In some cases, you may not be allowed to deduct the expense at all. Therefore, it is important to distinguish usual business expenses from expenses that include the following:
>
> - The expenses used to figure cost of goods sold.
> - Capital expenses.
> - Personal expenses.

text below comes from that publication.

The IRS goes on to explain each of the three categories in great detail. What is presented in this study are the highlights of the IRS discussion.

Capital Expenses

You must capitalize, rather than deduct, some costs. These costs are a part of your investment in your business and are called "capital expenses." Capital expenses are considered assets in your business. In general, you capitalize three types of costs.

- Business startup costs.
- Business assets.
- Improvements.

Cost recovery. Although you generally cannot take a current deduction for a capital expense, you may be able to recover the amount you spend through depreciation, amortization, or depletion. These recovery methods allow you to deduct part of your cost each year. In this way, you are able to recover your capital expense. See Amortization (chapter 8) and Depletion (chapter 9) in this publication.

Cost of Goods Sold
The following are types of expenses that go into figuring cost of goods sold.

- The cost of products or raw materials, including freight.
- Storage.
- Direct labor (including contributions to pension or annuity plans) for workers who produce the products.
- Factory overhead

Personal Expenses
Generally, you cannot deduct personal, living, or family expenses. However, if you have an expense for something that is used partly for business and partly for personal purposes, divide the total cost between the business and personal parts. You can deduct the business part.

These are the main ideas for capital expenses and the IRS makes it clear the costs can be deducted over a period of time. There are tables the IRS publishes that specifies these depreciation schedules.

After undertaking the computations to calculate net income, the income tax due is based on the level of income. The corporate tax rate was stable for years with the highest marginal tax rate for the large corporations at 35%. Shown below is the tax schedule for the years 1994 to 2012.

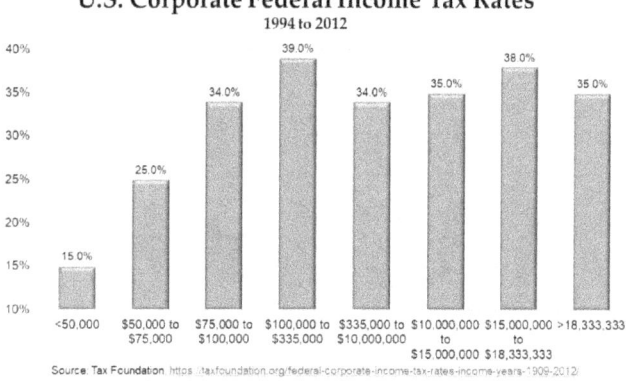

While the maximum marginal tax rate was 35%, estimates for the effective tax rates for corporations was much lower – often in the range of 15% to 20%. According to the Government Accountability Office or GAO, about 40% of all corporations paid no income tax. In its March 2016 report on Corporate Income Tax [see https://www.gao.gov/assets/680/675844.pdf] The GAO made the following statement.

> **What GAO Found**
> In each year from 2006 to 2012, at least two-thirds of all active corporations had no federal income tax liability. Larger corporations were more likely to owe tax. Among large corporations (generally those with at least $10 million in assets) less than half—42.3 percent—paid no federal income tax in 2012. Of those large corporations whose financial statements reported a profit, 19.5 percent paid no federal income tax that year. Reasons why even profitable corporations may have paid no federal tax in a given year include the use of tax deductions for losses carried forward from prior years and tax incentives, such as depreciation allowances that are more generous in the federal tax code than those allowed for financial accounting purposes.

This finding highlights a key issue, if such a large portion of U.S. corporations were not paying any federal income taxes, or paying taxes lower than the federal rate, why did the

Congress pass, and the President sign, the "Tax Acts and Jobs Act of 2017" that lowered the 35% marginal tax rates for large corporations to 21%?

From the GAO report we know tax incentives, loss carry-forward provisions and depreciation allowances were the main reasons profitable corporations did not pay federal income taxes. I want to discuss three topics regarding corporate taxation that are related to income inequality.

- Financial Engineering
- Corporate Tax Incentives
- Pass Through

Financial engineering has been going on for decades and involves corporations using funds to buy-back shares and pay dividends. On the surface, this may not seem related to inequality – but it is, from two perspectives. First, over 90% of the wealth in the United States is concentrated in the Top 20% households. Thus, this financial engineering directly benefits those who own these capital assets – and it is those in the top income quintile.

And second, corporations issue bonds and use the proceeds to buy-back shares and pay dividends. The interest paid on these bonds is a cost of doing business, which reduces corporate tax liability and taxes, is subsidized by other taxpayers thus increasing inequality, reduces government revenue and increases government debt. If corporations want to float bonds, they should – but the interest paid on those bonds should not be considered an "ordinary" cost of doing business. According the Harvard Business Review, "… the proportion of buybacks funded by corporate bonds reached as high as 30% in both 2016 and 2017." And according to the International Monetary Fund, these debt-funded stock repurchase programs are a form of financial risk-taking by U.S. companies that "can considerably weaken a firm's credit quality" [see *Global Financial Stability Report*, October 2019].

Thus, the first recommendation with regard to business taxes is that interest paid should ***not*** be deducted as a business expense. Keep in mind, the Tax Act of 2017 already put constraints on the portion of interest a company could deduct.

After the Tax Act of 2017, many companies had extra cash available for their operation because of the reduction in the top tax rate. There were many options companies had to spend the money – invest in new facilities, provide pay raises to rank and file employees, retire debt and so forth. What the vast majority of companies in the Standard & Poor's 500 chose to do with the extra cash was purchase more of their shares [repurchase programs] and pay higher dividends. According to the Harvard Business Review [see Why Stock Buybacks are Dangerous for the Economy," January 7, 2020], the cash buyback program of the large corporations totaled about $806 billion and set an all-time one-year record. This financial engineering helps the stock price [and thus those owning shares of the stock] but it does not help the firm expand or become more efficient. Again, the IMF believes these shares repurchase programs weaken a firm's credit quality.

Corporate Tax Incentives – In the GAO report, the authors listed tax incentives as one of the main reasons profitable companies did not pay taxes. Given that their effective tax rate is well below the 35% corporate tax rate, the second recommendation is to eliminate all these tax incentives.

The Pass Through. The third topic comes from the "Qualified Business Income Deduction" which is part of the Tax Cuts and Jobs Act of 2017. In this bill, individuals legally reduce their income tax liability on to the monies received from businesses [partnerships and S Corporations] by 20%. This pass-through deduction also applies to dividends paid by mortgage real estate investment trusts [mREIT]. Thus, this this pass through reduces tax liability for business owners as well as wealth holders. The third recommendation with regard to business taxes is that the Qualified Business Income Deduction" be removed from the tax code.

Depreciation. Eliminate depreciation – all of it. Capital expenditures can be deducted in the year in which they are made. The GAO report highlighted that deductions for depreciation was one area that was being abused. Rather than attempt to fix it, disallow all depreciation and have the write-off occur immediately.

The 21% Corporate Tax Rate. By reducing tax incentives, eliminating the interest rate deduction and depreciation, doing away with the 20% pass through and allowing all capital investments to be deducted immediately, the 21% corporate tax rate seems reasonable. Thus, the fourth recommendation is to maintain the corporate tax rate at 21%.

Historical Perspective

U.S. Personal Income grew significantly between 1979 and 2015 as shown in the chart below. The data in these charts are for total personal income and is not per household. Over time, the share of personal income from wages and salaries has decreased while income from government transfers, special income and other has increased. Special Income is the combination of LTCG, qualified dividends, interest from tax free municipal bonds and carried interest.

Between 2008 and 2009, the share of income from government transfers increased about 16% as unemployment insurance skyrocketed combined with business closures and layoffs due to the great recession. Partially motivated by losing their jobs, many "Baby Boomers" retired during this time and began collecting Social Security. At the same time, Special Income declined about 39% as banks failed, the stock market contracted and dividends paid were reduced.

112 | Historical Perspective

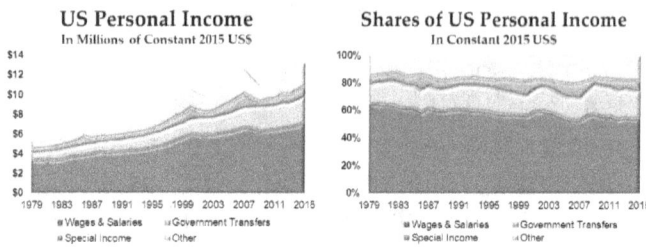

Since the number of households increased from about 78 million to 126 million between 1979 and 2015, this personal income data is divided by households to get a sense of what it was like for the "typical" household. Rather than use the entire data set, the information for the Middle Quintile is presented.

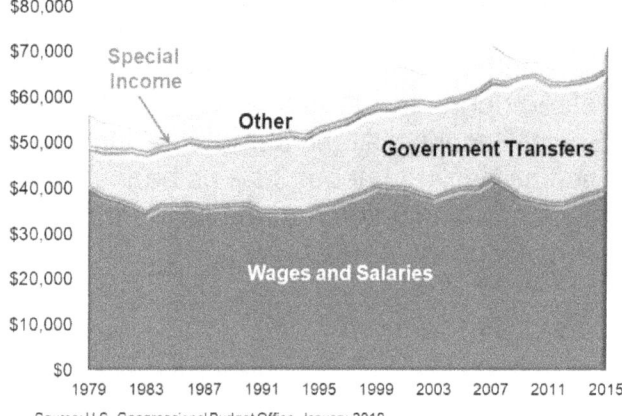

Historical Perspective | 113

Several points stand out from the data. First, average household income in constant 2015 US$ increased about 0.7% per year between 1979 and 2015. Second, the share of wages and salaries in the total is the largest component and declined steadily between 1979 and 2015 from about 71% in 1979 to about 56% in 2015. In the middle quintile household, real wages in 1979 were lower than real wages in 2015. And keep in mind that FICA taxes are only collected on Wages & Salaries.

Third, Government Transfers increased their share from about 15% in 1979 to about 36% in 2015. There was a large increase between 2008 and 2009 as the recession caused many to lose their jobs and collect unemployment compensation. Concurrently, many people at or near retirement began collecting social security. The share of household income from Government Transfers peaked in 2010 at about 40% and has declined since to about 36%. Looking forward, the Government Transfers portion could increase as more Baby Boomers retire and collect Social Security.

Fourth, Special Income is the smallest portion of income for the Middle Quintile and represents about 1% of Total Personal Income. The share varies significantly each year based on the

114 | Historical Perspective

performance of stocks. Between 1979 and 2015, the year with the highest share was 1.8% in 1997 and the low was 0.6% in 2009.

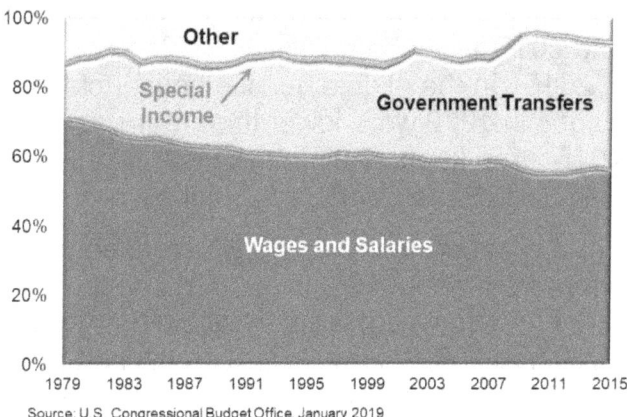

Shares of Middle Quintile Household Personal Income

Source: U.S. Congressional Budget Office, January 2019

Yet we know from the aggregate data that Special Income is about 8% of all income – so to get a clear view of Special Income, we examine this category by itself and divide it among the quintiles.

The top quintile receives the largest portion of income from this category – and they have done so for the entire period under investigation. Between 1979 and 2015, the top quintile received an average of 90+% of the Special Income category. In 2015, the top quintile had about 93% of Special Income, and remember, it is Special Income that has preferential tax rates.

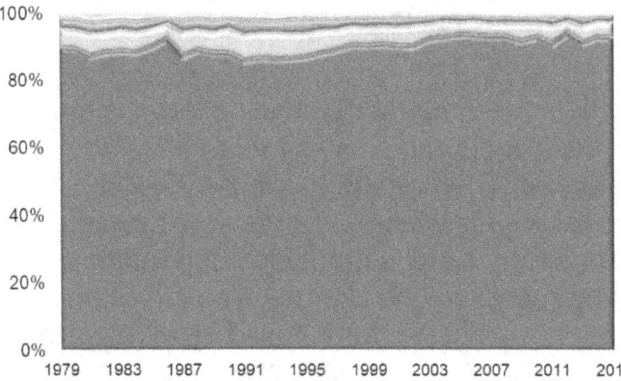

Shares of Special Income* By Quintile

■ Top Quintile ы Fourth Quintile ▣ Middle ⊔ Second Quintile ⊔ Lowest Quintile
* Composed of Long Term Capital Gains, Qualified Dividends, Carried Interest and Tax Free Bonds
Source: U.S. Congressional Budget Office, January 2019

Why does this category of income have special tax treatment? A cynic would answer that the wealthy can afford to hire lobbyists that write the tax code so there are preferential rates for the wealthy. This argument certainly has merit when referring to the component called Carried Interest.

Looking back at the 1913 income tax provision, the sale of homes [capital gains] was allowed to be taxed. In 1922, these capital gains were taxed at a lower rate compared to the marginal tax rate. Since then, capital gains have been taxed at various rates that tend to be lower than the marginal tax rate. Income from capital gains has averaged about 5% of personal income tax revenues according to the Congressional Research Service.

From a big picture economic perspective, the argument is made that having lower rates on LTCG encourages investors to have additional savings, which leads to greater capital investments which expands economic growth. However, there is no data to support this argument and the Congressional Research Service believes there would be no long-term impact from taxing Special Income the same as wages and salaries. In fact, we know that corporations can sell corporate bonds to raise cash for business expansion, or they can issue stock to raise capital that can be used for business expansion. There is no reason to think that raising individual income tax rates for qualified dividends or LTCG would lead to less capital investment.

Even investment experts think taxing Special Income at the marginal tax rates would have no impact on savings, capital investment and growth. In a wide-ranging interview on CNBC with the billionaire hedge fund manager Stanley Druckenmiller on June 7, 2019, Druckenmiller said: "I don't really think capital gains promote investment as much as advertised out there. It's hard for me to believe that Larry Page, Mark Zuckerberg and Jeff Bezos would have said, 'Oh my God, the capital gains is going to be 35% and I'm not going to be trying to found Amazon or Google.' So I don't have a problem with it [raising LTCG taxes]."

We have seen what income is like for the Middle Quintile, now let's examine income for each of the quintiles during the period 1979 to 2015.

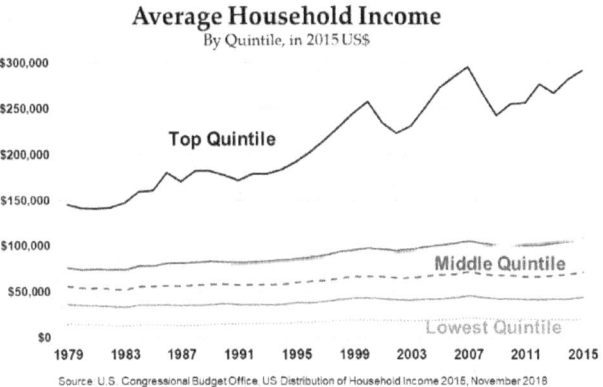

Looking at income levels since 1979 reveals almost flat incomes for the lowest three quintiles while real income in the upper quintile has doubled. Converting these dollar values to average annual income growth rates for the period highlights this fact.

Historical Perspective

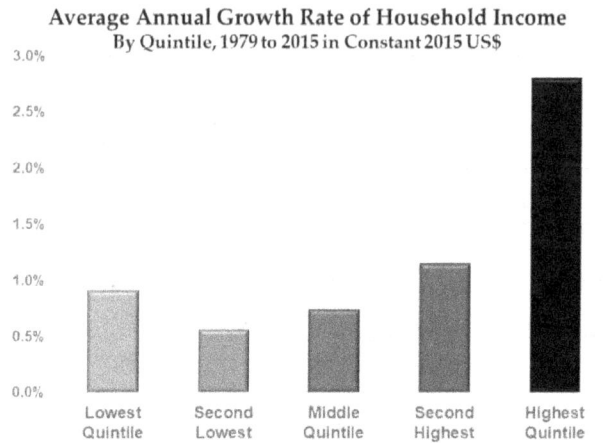

Source: U.S. Congressional Budget Office. US Distribution of Household Income 2015, November 2018

Sixty percent of American households had average annual growth of real incomes less than 1% per year between 1979 and 2015. In 2015, the average income for households in the lowest quintile was just above $20,000 per year and the average number of people in the household was 2½. The people in this group have difficulty obtaining health care, education and a host of other essentials.

Families in the second lowest quintile had an average income of just over $44,000 per year in 2015 with an average family size of 2½ people. For people in the lowest two quintiles – 40% of American households – there is limited discretionary income and these households face challenges when it comes to obtaining essentials such as health care and education. There are many young people in these households who will eventually be adults in the United States. I – for one – want our young people to be healthy and have a skill so they can be productive members of society. With such a large portion of the population having a difficult time with the basics, it does not portend well for the young people in these households.

In addition, almost 70% of U.S. Gross Domestic Product [GDP] comes from consumption. If 40% of the population can't afford many discretionary items, it limits the growth in demand for discretionary goods and services. And because of the slower growth, companies are reluctant to invest in the U.S. These same companies look for opportunities in areas where there is faster growth – and it is often outside the United States.

Part of the reason income inequality has worsened since 1979 is the growth in real incomes [incomes adjusted for inflation] for those at the very top. The chart below shows the growth in real incomes since 1993.

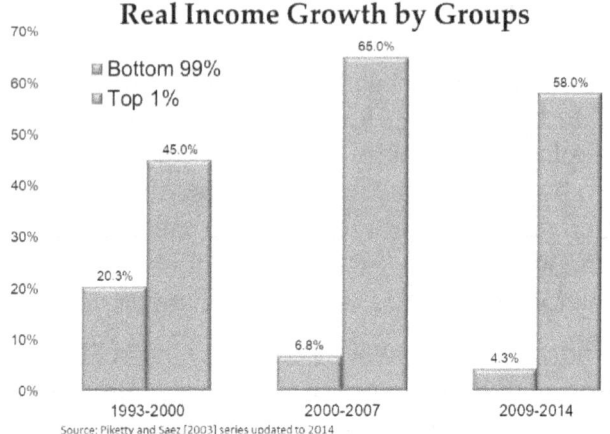

Since 2000, the vast majority of the economic growth has gone to the top 1% of income earners – amplifying inequality. Recent articles highlight this: A *USA Today* article on April 17, 2019 listed the CEO's of 13 major U.S. corporations that earned more than 1,000 times the median wage of their employees. All but one company was profitable and for 11 of the 13 companies, the median wage was between $5,000 and $18,000 per year. For Mattel, the one company that was not profitable, the median salary was $5,489 and the CEO pay was $18.7 million.

A recent article in *Time* magazine about the ride-sharing company Uber sums up what is occurring in the United States. According to the article, the CEO of Uber – Dara Khosrowshah –

earns $45 million per year while 40% of ride sharing drivers in New York City qualify for Medicaid [that means they are in the lowest income quintile]. The disparity is amazing. Many drivers work part-time and, according to the article, Uber drivers have seen their take home pay decline, while top management at Uber had their incomes skyrocket from the stock offering that occurred in May, 2019.

On June 6, 2019, one of the lead articles on CNN's home page was titled "Staggering Homelessness Count Stuns LA Officials" [see https://www.cnn.com/2019/06/05/politics/los-angeles-homeless-count/index.html].

Everywhere you turn it is becoming increasingly clear that the country is divided between the "haves" and the "have nots." If inequality continues to widen, my country [the USA] may face social upheaval as people's frustration and pain grows. The top five earners in the hedge fund industry all earned more than $1 billion per year in 2019 [*Market Insider*, "These are the Five Hedge-Fund Managers Who Took Home More than a Billion Dollars Last Year," February 11, 2020].

Another topic I wonder about: Why hasn't the federal minimum wage increased? The last increase was in July 2009 to $7.25 per hour –

where it stands today. More than 30 states have minimum wage rates which are greater than the federal standards, and some companies – such as Amazon – have raised the minimum wages they pay their employee regardless of the state. Even Walmart has increased the minimum wage it pays its employees by 50% over the last few years. What has prompted our federal government to ignore the low minimum wage? In many U.S. locations, the federal minimum wage is not a "living wage," which means employees being paid the minimum wage will not earn enough to meet minimum living standards for the local cost of living. If the minimum wage had kept up with the bonuses of Wall Street's financiers since 1985, it would currently be $33 per hour [see Inequality.org].

Over time, stagnant wages coupled with greater inequality led to frustration with the current economic system by many Americans. Many in US society believe they have been "left behind" during the US economic expansion. This frustration and their belief are two of the factors that helped propel Mr. Trump to the Presidency with his motto "Make America Great Again."

The tax revenue the federal government collects is related to those wages, so let's have a look at federal revenue.

U.S. Federal Government Revenue for 2019

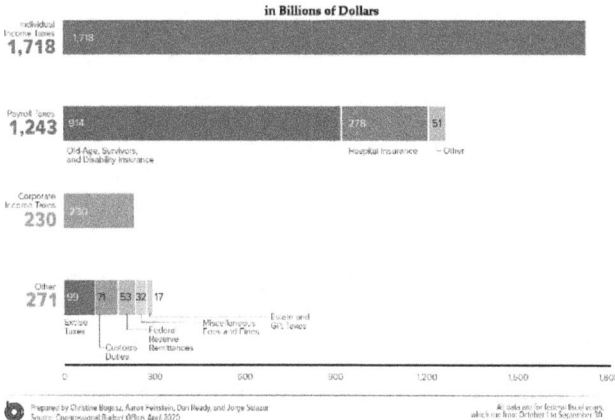

In 2019, the largest category of income was from individual income taxes and totaled about $1.7 trillion or 50% of all federal government revenues. Another $1.2 trillion or 36% came from payroll taxes. We know that payroll taxes are paid by both employees and employers. If we divide the payroll tax in half, we get a "rough" estimate of the payroll taxes paid by employees. And if we add the employee payroll tax with the individual income tax, we see that individuals account for about 68% of the federal government revenues. Corporations pay a relatively small portion of federal revenues through their income tax at about 7% of federal revenue. Now let's examine federal revenues over time.

124 | Historical Perspective

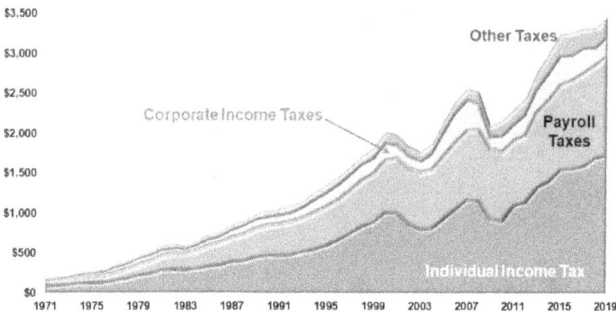

Revenues have grown with the economy and declined with a big dip in the early 2000s associated with the collapse of the dot com bubble and another dip during the great recession of 2008-2009 associated with the financial crisis. As noted earlier in this study, there have been far more income tax reductions than income tax increases. So, it appears the growth seen in this chart has been reduced by recessions and tax law changes that reduced tax rates. Now let's look at the distribution of revenue by source over time.

Shares of U.S. Government Tax Revenue

Source: Office of Management and Budget, Historical Tables, Table 2.3, see https://www.whitehouse.gov/omb/historical-tables

Here we see that individual income tax revenue – as a share of total revenue – has remained fairly constant over time – with a slight uptick in the last two years. Recessions put downward pressure on all the tax sources. But income tax changes have caused the largest alterations. In particular, the Tax Act of 2017 significantly reduced the corporate income tax rate, which led to less corporate revenue and increased the share from individual income taxes – even though the individual income tax rates were reduced. The corporate tax share was 9.0% in 2017, 6.1% in 2018 [the first year of the lower tax rates] and 6.7% in 2019.

To examine revenue as a share of Gross Domestic Product or GDP, we now plot the three major categories over time.

126 | Historical Perspective

Between 1979 and 2015 there was a great deal of variation in individual income tax receipts as a share of GDP. The low occurred in 2010 when the share was 6.1% and this was at the time of the great recession and many people suffered job losses and reduced income. The peak occurred in 2000 when the share was 9.9% and this is associated with the dot com bubble when many people had capital gains from a soaring stock market. For the entire period, the average individual income tax share was 8.0% of GDP. For 2019 – the most recent year – the share was 8.1%.

Between 1979 and 2015, the average share of Corporate Income Taxes as a share of GDP was 1.9%. The peak occurred in 1973 when the share was 2.7% and the low occurred in two years: 2009 and in 2018 at 1.0%. For 2019 – the most recent year – the share was 1.1%.

Payroll taxes as a share of GDP seem more stable than either Individual Income Taxes or Corporate Income Taxes. As a share of GDP payroll taxes averaged 5.9% with a low of 5.1% in 1974 and a high of 6.1% in 2001. For 2019 – the most recent year – the share was 5.9%.

And what of the federal government debt – how has it faired during this period? The charts below are from the U.S. Congressional Budget Office [CBO] who published a "primer" on Federal debt in March 2020. If you have not seen this publication, I encourage you to visit the CBO website and download the report. See https://www.cbo.gov/publication/56165 .

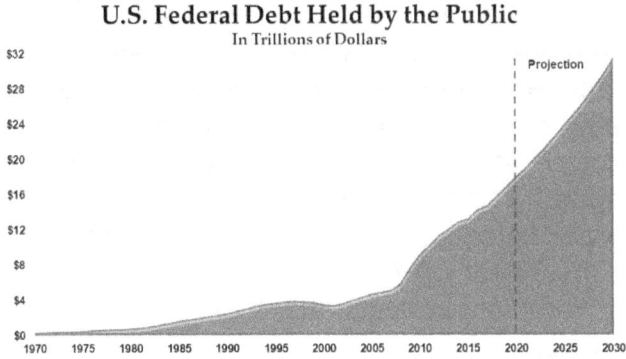

U.S. Federal Debt Held by the Public
In Trillions of Dollars

Source: U.S. Congressional Budget Office, "Federal Debt: A Primer", March, 2020

Historical Perspective

The historical data reveal a steady upward climb since the great recession of 2008. With the passage of the Tax Act of 2017, the rate of the increase in federal debt continued to increase and the CBO projected a skyrocketing federal debt through 2030. The $2.4 trillion Coronavirus Aid, Relief, and Economic Security (CARES) Act was enacted in March 2020 – after the CBO Debt Primer was published – and will accelerate the level of debt held by the U.S. In fact, prior to the CARES Act, the 2020 deficit was projected at about $1 trillion. With the CARES Act and other supplemental funding, the likely U.S. Federal Government deficit will be larger than $3 trillion.

Converting this debt data to a ratio of debt to GDP shows a similar pattern. In 2007 – just before the financial crisis – the debt to GDP ratio was about 35%. With the advent of the great recession the ratio soared to 52% by 2009, and then went to 76% by 2012. The current ratio stands at about 80% and will approach 100% of GDP by 2030. Again, this projection occurred before the pandemic and subsequent CARES Act enacted by the government in March 2020.

With the CARES Act passed in 2020, the estimated debt/GDP ratio for the United States

Historical Perspective | 129

in 2020 is about 122% – similar to the U.S. ratio at the end of World War II.

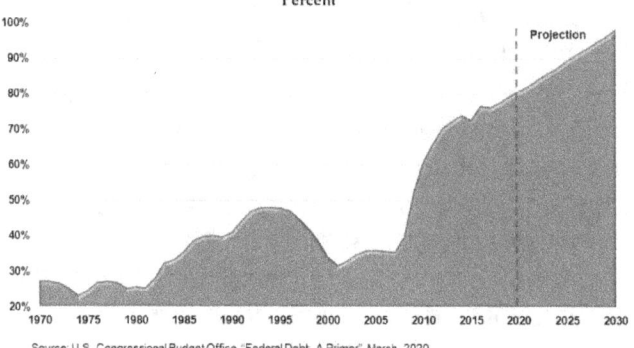

U.S. Federal Debt as a Share of Gross Domestic Product
Percent

Source: U.S. Congressional Budget Office, "Federal Debt: A Primer", March, 2020

To summarize, inequality has increased substantially since 1974. Most of the income growth between 1979 and 2015 accrued to the top quintile. The tax code favors the wealthy by providing lower tax rates for income from wealth – and that wealth is primarily held by the top 10%. Further, the government has promoted greater income inequality through its policies of providing tax incentives to large corporations, reducing taxes on the wealthy while reducing expenditures on services such as health care to help the lowest quintile. The combination of subsidies and lower tax rates are causing a massive increase in U.S. debt and the debt to GDP ratio is higher than any time since WW II.

Historical Perspective

Not only do current policies increase inequality in our population, they put our country at risk in the future as it is burdened with an ever-increasing level of debt – both in absolute terms, and as a share of GDP.

The infographic on the next page captures the relationship between inequality and the highest marginal personal income tax rate, the highest marginal personal income tax rate and economic growth, and the highest marginal personal income tax rate and the United States debt to GDP ratio. All of these factors are intertwined and presented in this single graphic.

Historical Perspective | 131

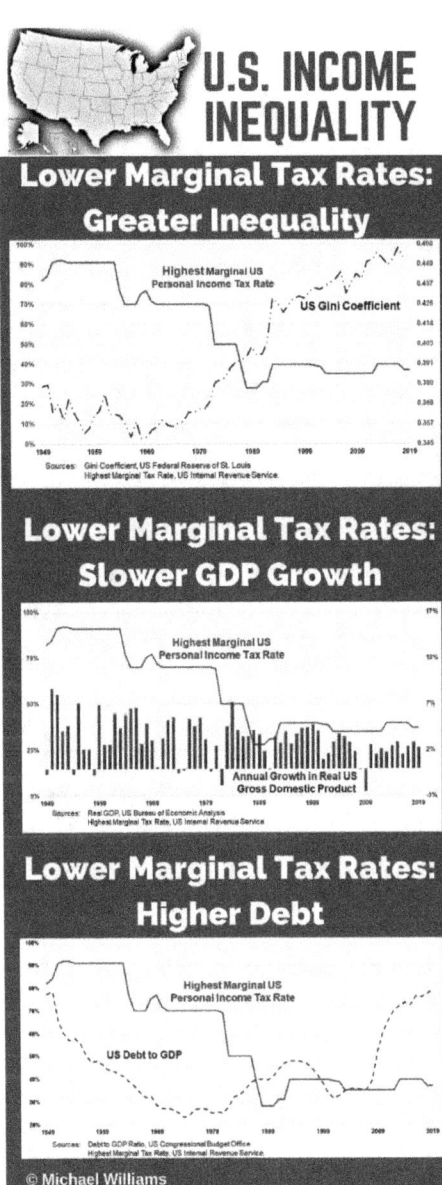

Comparing the Current Tax System with The Proposals

I began this book by stating that the underlying emphasis of my work is to lessen income inequality, eliminate preferential tax treatment, broaden the tax base, and simplify the tax code. I also went to The Constitution and drew from the Preamble where it states "... promote the general welfare ..." from which I obtained my emphasis on health and education. These ideas guided me as I reviewed our tax system.

Personal Income Taxes

Individual Income Tax Comparison: Current System & Proposals

	Tax Rates	
	Current	Proposed
Lowest	10%	10%
	12%	12%
	22%	22%
	24%	24%
	32%	32%
	35%	35%
Highest	37%	**40%**
Itemization	Allow	Eliminate
Standard Deduction		
Individual	$12,200	$18,300
Married, Joint	$24,000	$36,000
Married, Separate	$12,200	$18,300
Head of Household	$18,350	$27,525
A M T	Yes	Eliminate
Preferential Income Tax Rates		
LTCG	0%-15%-20%	Eliminate
Qualified Dividends	0%-15%-20%	Eliminate
Carried Interest	0%-15%-20%	Eliminate
Tax Free Bonds	0%	Eliminate

With regard to the tax rates, recall that they are the same for all categories of filers [single, married filing jointly, married filing separately, and head of household]. What is different for the four categories is the level of income for each tax bracket. The only change recommended for the tax rates is to raise the top income bracket tax rate to 40% from 37%. A top rate of 40% compares quite favorably with the 90% top tax rate that was operational in the 1950s when economic growth averaged more than 4% for the entire decade. It is recommended that the revenue from this increase be divided between funding for Medicaid and funding for higher education.

Eliminating itemization provides fairness and simplifies the tax code. During the congressional negotiations for itemization for the Tax Act of 2017, the initial proposal was to eliminate itemization. Itemization was eventually allowed with reduced allowances for mortgage interest and state and local taxes [SALT]. The idea to eliminate mortgage interest deductions is not new. After the 2008-2009 recession, hearings in Congress were held on the mortgage interest deductions and the manner in which it encouraged overleveraging by households. During the July 13, 2011 hearings in Congress, it was recommended by the Peterson Institute for International Economics to reduce the incentives for household overleveraging, i.e., phaseout the mortgage interest deduction over time. Since the Tax Act of 2017 reduced the amount of mortgage interest and SALT deductions, this recommendation to eliminate itemization is a follow up to the Tax Act of 2017 and the recommendations from 2011.

Increasing the Standard Deduction by 50% in conjunction with eliminating itemization helps put everyone on the same footing. The Tax Act of 2017 eliminated personal exemptions – which impacted lower income households more than upper income households. Increasing the Standard Deduction also helps to offset the loss of personal exemptions.

Eliminating the Alternative Minimum Tax [AMT] would simplify the tax code and make everyone's life a little easier with the exception of tax accountants.

Eliminating Preferential Tax Rates is needed to restore a sense of fairness to the income tax system and simplify the system. Much of the frustration with the current system is its complexity and the fact that those with higher incomes pay a smaller effective income tax rate than those with lower income.

Individual Payroll Taxes

Payroll Tax Comparison: Current System & Proposals

	Current	Proposed
Social Security		
Earned Income	6.2%	6.2%
Income Limits	$137,700	$137,700
Non-Earned Income	0.0%	6.2%
Income Limits	$0	$137,700
Employer Match	N / A	None
Medicare		
Earned Income	1.45%	1.45%
Income Limits	None	None
NIIT	2.35%	2.35%
Non-Earned Income	$0	1.45%
Income Limits	N / A	None
Employer Match	N / A	None
Medicaid		
Earned Income	N / A	N / A
Non-Earned Income	None	1.45%
Income Limits	N / A	None
Employer Match	None	None
Education		
Earned Income	N / A	N / A
Non-Earned Income	None	2.00%
Income Limits	N / A	None
Employer Match	None	None

The main emphasis for much of this is to treat all income equally. Many in the upper income strata already pay preferential tax rates and do not pay payroll taxes on significant portions of their income that are not earned such as "Special Income," ordinary interest, ordinary dividends and short-term capital gains. The categories of "Special Income" are Long term Capital Gains, Carried Interest, Qualified Dividends and interest from Tax-Free Municipal Bonds. To help fund programs that reduce poverty [Social Security] and fund health care and education, the payroll taxes outlined in these proposals are dedicated to programs designed to help the less well off. What is being suggested is that all non-earned income [including "Special Income"] be taxed like ordinary income and the payroll taxes be applied to non-earned income and earmarked for their respective programs. You will also note that the Net Investment Income Tax or NIIT is not eliminated.

For these taxes it should also be kept in mind that about 90% of all wealth is held by the top quintile. Historically, payroll taxes have been regressive [lower incomes pay higher rates] and this proposal should make payroll taxes less regressive as the wealth holders will be the primary individuals paying these taxes.

Business Taxes

Business Tax Comparison: Current System & Proposals

	Current	Proposed
Maximum Tax Rate	21%	21%
Allowable Business Expenses		
Interest	Yes	Eliminate
Depreciation	Yes	Eliminate
Capital Investments		
Depreciate	Yes	Eliminate
Immediate Expense	No	Yes
20% Pass Through	Yes	Eliminate
A M T	Yes	Eliminate
Tax Incentives	Yes	Eliminate

About 20% of large business do not pay corporate income tax and the US General Accountability Office [GAO] noted this in their 2016 report. Among the reasons they did not pay taxes included mis-use of depreciation, loss carry-forward, and other tax incentives. Given that corporations now face a 21% maximum tax rate, it seems reasonable to eliminate incentives and items that the corporations have used to "game" the tax system when the tax rate was 35%.

From an inequality perspective, it is known that a significant portion of interest from corporate bonds has been used to repurchase shares and pay dividends. Since the top quintile owns about 90% of the wealth in the United States, these share repurchase programs exacerbate inequality. To this end I recommend that all interest be eliminated as an ordinary and necessary expense. And it should also be recalled that the Tax Act of 2017 put limits on the amount of interest deductions – so this recommendation follows up on that Act.

Finally, the 20% Pass through that is part of the Tax Cuts and Jobs Act of 2017 also amplifies inequality by providing a 20% tax reduction for the wealthiest. It is recommended that this be eliminated.

The Nature of Big Business in the United States

One of the bedrocks of U.S. business is free markets with some regulations, but mostly market oriented activities of the companies. The concept of shareholder value became important in the 1980s and is associated with General Electric's former president Jack Welch. "Shareholder Value" is defined by Investopedia as the following:

> "Shareholder value is the value delivered to the equity owners of a corporation due to management's ability to increase sales, earnings, and free cash flow, which leads to an increase in dividends and capital gains for the shareholders.
>
> A company's shareholder value depends on strategic decisions made by its board of directors and senior management, including the ability to make wise investments and generate a healthy return on invested capital. If this value is created, particularly over the long term, the share price increases and the company can pay larger cash dividends to shareholders. Mergers, in particular, tend to cause a heavy increase in shareholder value."

The emphasis on shareholder value became a driving force for large corporations. Before delving into aspects of shareholder value, it is important to remember who the shareholders are. They are primarily the top quintile of households as 90+% of all wealth in the United States is held by them. Further, the president and other senior staff of large corporations are shareholders of major corporations. Often the senior staff have an significant portion of their remuneration paid to them in stock options. For senior staff, shareholder value is not an idle concept, but an integral part of their pay.

So, what can be done to increase shareholder value? One aspect is to improve profitability. Since labor is a key component of any operation, reducing labor costs can be accomplished by having more efficient operations and fewer or less expensive employees. This can be accomplished by substituting capital for labor and substituting lower cost labor for higher cost labor. In the case of substituting lower cost labor for higher cost labor, a company can do this by subcontracting with individuals as opposed to hiring them as employees. Another option is to sponsor low cost labor from foreign nations to work in the United States. For highly skilled positions, this is one way of obtaining the skills at a lower cost. And finally, corporations can hire younger employees to do the same job as older employees. The corporation can offer "early retirement" to the older employees with a financial package for the incentive. When the older employee takes the offer, a younger, less expensive employee is substituted.

All of these options to reduce labor cost have something in common – the individual is viewed as a cost center and – in the name of shareholder value – the individual is sacrificed to improve profitability. This has happened over decades to thousands of individuals. These individuals may continue to work for the same company, but lose their employment status, or they may get laid off and find employment at another firm – at a lower salary.

Corporations also help keep labor costs under control by attempting to limit membership in unions. According to Wikipedia, membership in U.S. unions peaked in 1983 at 17.7 million people and stood at 14.6 million members in 2019. In the private sector, 6.2% of employees are union members compared to over 33% in the public sector. The big corporations have taken a multi-pronged approach to control labor costs – and they have succeeded.

The U.S. Congress has been an active participant in reducing corporate labor costs by keeping the minimum wage at its current level of $7.25 per hour since July 2009. The Senate majority leader has voted numerous times over several decades to reject increasing the minimum wages saying it would cause layoffs. With 40 million people losing their jobs in 2020, this statement rings hollow.

Another way to increase shareholder value is to increase dividends. And a corporation does not have to increase profitability to do so. They can sell bonds on the market and use the proceeds to repurchase shares and pay dividends. This is what Apple and many large corporations have done. In the *Wall Street Journal* on February 16, 2016, Tim Cook [the President of Apple] announced that the company would sell $12 billion worth of bonds to fund the repurchase of shares and pay dividends. Further, if a company purchases shares on the open market, and its profitability does **NOT** change, the dividend per share increases as there are fewer shares. This is the financial engineering mentioned earlier in this study. Recall the IMF stated that these repurchase plans do not make a company stronger but decrease their credit quality by increasing their risk.

Shareholder value has seen corporations take on more risk to increase profitability and increase shareholder value. This was part of the driving force for some of the banks just prior to the financial collapse. In fact, it was their risk taking that contributed to the financial disaster in 2008-2009. Afterwards there were bailouts to companies that helped create the disaster and this brought the wrath of a political group who named themselves the "Tea Party." They thought government should be smaller.

It was after the great recession that John Stiglitz coined the phrase "privatize profits and socialize losses," referring to the fact that companies would take large risks and gain all the rewards, and when there was a disaster, the government would bail them out. In an interview on CNBC on March 17, 2010, the Nobel laureate said "Today, (at) most of the big companies you have managers who, when things go well, walk off with a lot of money. When things go bad the shareholders bear the costs. It's a system where you socialize the losses and privatize the gains, which is not capitalism ... There is moral hazard everywhere," he said. Regarding regulation, Stiglitz went on to say: "... it's hard to find any evidence from anybody ... that can show any clear link between the so-called financial innovations and increased productivity in our economy." Instead of creating products to manage risks, the financial markets created new products that increased risks, he added.

Our elected officials in Washington believe in Shareholder Value. In doing so they implicitly ignore the public welfare and focus on corporate welfare. Over time this focus has continued to erode the financial strength of the U.S. government [by continually lowering taxes and increasing debt] and this focus weakens U.S. institutions designed to help individuals succeed. Some recent examples include removing water pollution regulations to increase coal production, attempting to reduce Medicaid support for the less well-off and attempting to reduce social security and Medicare for the elderly to help balance the U.S. budget after some large tax cuts to corporations and wealthy individuals. These are aspects that accelerate income inequality and slow economic growth.

While listening to CNBC on a weekday during the April 2020 pandemic, it was clear the moderator could not understand why the stock market and the real economy were not synchronized. That is to say, if the stock market increased, the growth rate in the real economy should increase. This institutionalization of shareholder value in our lexicon is taken for granted and it is assumed to be integrated as part of the real economy that produces goods or services.

The bailout packages from the great recession in 2008, and the Tax Act of 2017 primarily supported business. Several examples from the CARES Act in 2020 highlight this. First, the funding for state and local governments that provide health care services to handle pandemic cases received less than half the funding allocated to small business. While individuals will eventually receive payments for short-term dislocations, those in the lower strata will likely receive them much later than those in the middle strata.

And the CARES Act of 2020 also amplifies inequality. Hidden away in the Act of 2020 is a provision for $80 billion for real estate developers called "Modification of Limitation on Losses for Taxpayers Other Than Corporations" and more than 80% of the revenue would go to 43,000 taxpayers with income greater than $1 million – this would include the President of the United States and his children [see the letter from the Joint Tax Commission to Senator Whitehouse and Mr. Doggett, dated April 9, 2020 dealing with this topic]. It might be difficult to acquire the names of the recipients of these monies as the Inspector General responsible for monitoring the distribution of the CARES funds was fired by the President.

What is missing is consideration for the long-term health and well-being of the ordinary individual – not the millionaire. The debate and discussion on the $2 trillion bailout for the pandemic of 2020 often pitted those who wanted greater benefits for the individual versus those who wanted greater leniency for businesses. It seems as if everyone touts the superiority of capitalism. Yet those same capitalists want preferential tax treatment, and they want to get federal aid when there are problems – like during the recession of 2008-2009 – which was brought on – in part – by the large financial corporations. In the Coronavirus Aid, Relief, and Economic Security (CARES) Act, Congress allocated over $50 billion to "bail-out" the airline industry but only $150 billion to state and local governments that lost billions due to the economic downturn and are funding the fight against the coronavirus. In fact, the Center on Budget Policy and Priorities estimates state governments will have a shortfall of about $435 billion in 2020 and 2021 [see "States Continue to Face Large Shortfalls Due to COVID-19 Effects," June 15, 2020]. To put these data into perspective, I compare the CARES relief funds per employee of five airlines that received funding to the allocation to state and local governments.

Employment and Financial Allocations
Coronavirus Air, Relief and Economic Security [CARES] Act

	5 Major Airlines	State & Local Government
Employees	351,076	7,716,710
CARES	$ 15,606,000,000	$150,000,000,000
CARES / Employee	**$44,452**	**$19,438**

Notes: Government employment excludes schools and hospitals
Airlines: American, Delta, United, Alaska, Hawaii

Sources: CARES Act, Bloomberg, U.S. Bureau of Labor Statistics
Airline web pages

From this simple analysis we see the five large airline corporations receive more than two times the bailout money per employee than what is budgeted for state and local governments, noting that the data for state and local governments excludes employees at schools and hospitals.

These same airline companies engaged in financial engineering during the previous decade to increase their shareholder value. In fact, the companies spent more than two times the value of their CARES funds on stock repurchases.

Airlines Cash Flow, Stock Buybacks & CARES FUNDING
Cash Flow and Buybacks for 10 Years Ending December 32, 2019

	Free Cash Flow Billions US$	Stock Buybacks Billions US$	Share	CARES Funding Billions US$	Ratio
American	-7.935	12.957	N/A	5.810	2.23
Delta	23.186	11.430	49%	5.400	2.12
United	11.526	8.883	77%	2.750	3.23
Alaska	4.948	1.590	32%	0.992	1.60
Total	31.725	34.860		14.952	
Average			110%		2.33

Sources: CARES Act, Bloomberg, MarketWatch

For the airlines for which data are readily available from articles, their CARES funding totaled $14.95 billion while their expenditures during the previous decade on stock buybacks totaled $34.86 billion. Why didn't these firms reduce their debt? Or expand production capacity? Or, do something to improve their long-term viability? In June 2020, after receiving $5.8 billion under the CARES Act, American Airlines decided to issue an addition $3.5 billion in debt for their operation. Why didn't they do this prior to getting the CARES bailout? And after October 1, these airlines are free to reduce the size of their workforce without any repercussions to the funds they received from the bailout [see CNBC, "Airline Employees' Dilemma: Take Severance or Gamble on Oct. 1 Layoffs," June 10, 2020].

The U.S. company Amazon continually invests in new ventures and has been criticized for not being more profitable. Yet during the pandemic of 2020, the Amazon stock price increased because the company positioned itself to be essential to many of its customers. Amazon does not rely on the U.S. government for a bailout – and perhaps other large corporations need to take note and not plan on a bailout during a crisis.

If that were not enough, the Associate Press uncovered the fact that some publicly traded companies with a market capitalization greater than $100 million received funds under the small business loan package [see https://apnews.com/6c5942eec36cc43b25ad5df5afebcfbd].

During the congressional debate on additional funding for state and local governments, it was the Senate Majority leader who said "I would certainly be in favor of allowing states to use the bankruptcy route. It saves some cities. And there's no good reason for it not to be available." See the *New York Times*, "McConnell Says States Should Consider Bankruptcy, Rebuffing Calls for Aid," April 22, 2020.

The Senate Majority Leader supports legislation that improves shareholder value and the value of his portfolio. He does not support legislation for governments that provide health care and education.

In fact, Larry Kudlow, the White House Economic Advisor during the pandemic of 2020, suggested that the corporate income tax rates be reduced by 50% for moving production to the United States [see Reuters, "White Houses' Kudlow Floats Cutting Corporate Tax Rate in Half", May 15, 2020]. Another example of the U.S. government finding ways to help increase shareholder value.

Since 1986 I would say the large corporations and wealthy have succeeded in obtaining federal funds at the expense of public services. They see shareholder value as the highest priority.

And it is not. Shareholder value has amplified income inequality and made our country weaker.

Beyond Taxes

The challenges facing the United States in 2020 go beyond tax rates. While having a transparent and simple income tax system would go a long way to instilling a sense of fairness and trust, a call to action is needed – NOW – to try and reverse the 50-year trend of worsening U.S. inequality. My fear is that continued deteriorating of inequality will cause increases in frustration and civil unrest.

There are two major areas where government action taken today can improve the situation. These are raising the minimum wage and instituting a jobs program. Each of these is now discussed.

Minimum Wage

It has been 11 years since July 2009 when the U.S. Federal minimum wage was set at $7.25 per hour. In January 2020, 29 states and the District of Columbia had a minimum wage higher than the Federal standard. The idea of raising the minimum wage is not new; it has been implemented by state governments around the country, and by many corporations. Why has the Federal government failed to increase the minimum wage?

From my perspective, the reason is that the majority of elected officials believe in shareholder value, are millionaires, and own shares in U.S. corporations. The estimated net worth of the Senate Majority leader during the pandemic of 2020 is more than $20 million and he has voted against raising the minimum wage many times over decades. The Senate Majority Leader said raising the minimum wage would cause jobs to be lost – he does not consider that 40 million jobs were lost during the pandemic. And I believe he sees a higher minimum wage as reducing corporate profits and his shareholder value.

Jobs Program

Similar to the Civilian Conservation Corp [CCC] founded by President Franklin Delano Roosevelt in 1933, our country needs a job program. The program could have two [2] major components:

1. **Coronavirus Testing and Tracing** – people could be hired to conduct large scale testing of individuals and tracing their contacts to help our medical system better fight the virus.

2. **Infrastructure Development and Repair** – this would repair and improve our nation's infrastructure to include such

things as roads, bridges, airports, ship ports, sewer systems, internet connectivity, waste disposal, schools, clean energy production and the like. Our country's infrastructure has been rated a D by the American Society of Civil Engineers for decades and much of it was constructed by the CCC during the 1930s. There are so many things that could be done to improve our nation. I suggest you read the most recent report at https://www.infrastructurereportcard.org/ and get a sense of how bad the U.S. infrastructure is, and the broad array of things that are in poor condition. Apart from the poor infrastructure, the idea of preparing our nation for 2050 through improvements in the use and distribution of technology while implementing a sustainable development strategy is paramount. The International Energy Agency published a special report in June 2020 that offers recommendations for a sustainable recovery. There are recommendations for electricity, transport, buildings, industry and fuels and you can download the report at https://www.iea.org/reports/sustainable-recovery . This can be a time when the U.S. government uses this calamity to move our nation forward. Both the IEA report and Infrastructure report provide estimates of the increase in GDP associated with their recommendations.

In May 2020 the House of Representatives was considering more funds to help combat the pandemic. What is **not** needed is more spending money for citizens or more bailouts for large corporations. What is needed is jobs and the U.S. Federal government has the opportunity to begin hiring and training people to get them back to work, make them more productive and prepare our country for the next 50 years.

Apart from the fact that people would have more money, their skill development would go beyond just the pandemic and put them in a trajectory to have a living wage and a possible career path. At the same time, a sense of self-worth could be restored, our infrastructure could be repaired and upgraded, and better opportunities could become available to the disenfranchised.

Conclusions

I think the issue boils down to what we want for our society and our country. Do we want a society where everyone has the opportunity to be healthy, productive and contribute to the country's growth and prosperity? Or do we want a country that maintains the king and his court while a significant portion of our population are living on an income level that does not support good heath or the development of skills?

At the World Economic Forum [WEF] in January 2020, the WEF presented a paper titled "The Global Social Mobility Report 2020, Quality, Opportunity and a New Economic Imperative." Some noteworthy comments on page 5 include:

- "Low wages, lack of social protection and poor lifelong learning systems are the greatest challenges globally."
- "The economic and social returns from investing in the right mix of social mobility factors are substantial… If countries … were to improve their social mobility index score by 10 points, this would result in an additional GDP growth of 4.41% by 2030 in addition to vast social cohesion benefits."

- "A new financing model for social mobility is necessary through taxation but must be complemented by a new mix of spending and tailored approaches."

The WEF explains social mobility as multi-dimensional and includes inter and intra-generational social-economic mobility, income mobility, and educational mobility. And – of the 82 countries in the study – the U.S. is ranked 27th. Most of the countries at the top of the list were Scandinavian where health and education are provided to all citizens at no cost. The WEF lists pillars for global mobility and the top spot is health, next is education [which includes access, quality and lifelong learning], next is access to technology, next is fair opportunities for work [which includes wages and working conditions] and last is social protection. Thinking back on some of the protests that occurred in the U.S. after George Floyd was killed on May 25, 2020, the protestors were asking for fairness, social protection and institutional inclusion.

Will the U.S. move towards increasing equality and social mobility? Hearings before the Committee on the Budget in the House of Representatives were held during early 2019 and provide insights on the thinking of some of our elected officials. The Director of the

The Nature of Big Business in the United States | 161

Congressional Budget Office [CBO] Keith Hall attended and answered questions about the economy, the federal budget and the federal deficit. In notes from the Chairman dated February 5, 2019, the following is learned: "Throughout the hearing, Republicans reiterated their goal of cutting vital programs in order to reduce the deficits their tax cuts exacerbated. While CBO projects rising spending on Social Security and health care programs will drive increases in government outlays going forward, Republicans' proposed solution – slashing Social Security, Medicare, and Medicaid – shows a fundamental misunderstanding of the problem."

Since taking office in 2017, the current administration has promoted the repeal of the American Healthcare Act, reduced the preparedness of the Center for Disease Control, reduced the amount of food aid available to lower income people, reduced financial support for students to go to college, reduced regulations that prohibited companies from dumping toxic waste that would affect groundwater, and reduced the amount of land in protected areas to allow greater development by private companies. All of these things reduce the ability of lower income individuals to succeed and prosper. Remember, lower income people often live nearer areas that are environmentally damaged – which can cause related health issues and affect productivity.

Part of the reason inequality has worsened is due to the tax treatment of income with the concurrent reduction in programs to help those in the lower quintiles. Wealthy individuals have lobbied for years – and succeeded – in getting lower tax rates for their income categories. The argument of many – including Larry Kudlow, the President's Chief Economic Advisor, is that raising taxes will slow economic growth – and there is scant evidence to support this. The U.S. Congress raised taxes in 1993 and several things happened after the tax increase. Economic growth [as measured by annual increases in real GDP] averaged 4.0% per year from 1994 through 2000 and the deficit declined and turned positive for four years before another tax decrease was passed in 2001 – after which economic growth declined and the government began incurring deficits. The idea that higher taxes slows economic growth is supported by the wealthy legislators voted into office in the U.S. Congress, and the President. It is not supported by fact.

This has also led to some very wealthy people paying a lower tax rate than their employees. In an opinion article for the *New York Times*,

Warren Buffet wrote in 2011 "While the poor and middle-class fight for us in Afghanistan, and while most Americans struggle to make ends meet, we mega-rich continue to get our extraordinary tax breaks."

This preferential tax treatment expanded under "The Tax Cuts and Jobs Act of 2017" which President Trump signed into law by lowering the top rate for individuals to 37% and providing a 20% deduction for "qualified business income." These new benefits are in addition to lower tax rates for long-term capital gains, qualified dividends, carried interest and interest from tax-free municipal bonds. These new tax breaks reduced federal government income and increased the annual federal government deficit to about $780 billion in FY 2018 and is expected to increase the deficit to about $1 trillion in FY 2019. With the CARES Act of 2020, the government deficit could surpass $3 trillion.

Preferential tax treatment for those at the very top amplifies the distrust many have with the taxation system. And the findings in April that 43,000 households would receive $1.6 million under the CARES Act [while most received $1,200] only amplified the mistrust and sense that the system is rigged. The newly elected congressional representatives of 2018 began articulating changes to the tax code to help make it fairer. Some new representatives suggested a tax rate of 70% of income over $10 million while others have promoted a wealth tax. The news media focused on this and many pundits stated that returning to historically high-income tax rates would reduce economic growth and cause a collapse in the US economy. These pundits overlooked the era of the 1950s when the highest individual tax rate averaged more than 90% and US economic growth averaged 4.3% for the years 1950 to 1959. The average economic growth rate for that decade is higher than any individual year since 2000.

These statistics miss a very important point – the individual. With high inequality, individuals in lower income brackets have a more difficult time obtaining health care and advancing their labor skills – both of which are vital to make them productive members of society. The pandemic of 2020 has amplified the inequality that was in place prior to its arrival and has put many in the lowest quintile at greater risk of contracting the virus. Remember, it is the lower income individuals that are often on the front lines working in restaurants, collecting garbage, working in food processing plants and other jobs where they are more likely to contract the coronavirus. High income workers have the luxury of working on their computers at their home. This inequality can also be defined by those with higher education versus those with less education.

If we want our future leaders to be healthy and wise, we – as a country – need to provide them with access to both health care and education. Since there is no such thing as a free lunch, these benefits need to be funded from revenue and this study offers some insights and recommendations on personal federal income taxes, payroll taxes and corporate income taxes that will help "level the playing field" for all taxpayers while increasing revenue for programs to help those in lower income brackets become productive members of society.

A Note on Methodology

I wanted to present the basic tax system without getting bogged down in details that alter the exact tax rate, but don't change the concept. Given the complexity of the tax system, this was a challenge. A good example is compiling a time series of tax rates for the maximum and minimum individual tax rates, and the maximum long-term capital gains tax rate. I did not always use the summary data presented, but used the number found in tax tables or the IRS instructions. The reason I did this was because adjustment to tax rates based on the phaseout of deductions, the alternative minimum tax, or some other reason could alter the rate – but they would not alter the basic idea. To illustrate this complexity, I have copied and inserted the footnotes from the U.S. Internal Revenue Service document containing long term capital gains tax rates.

The IRS Note

The maximum rate is the effective rate applying to high-income taxpayers, including provisions that alter effective rates for significant amounts of gains. Maximum rates include the effects of exclusions (1954- 86), alternative tax rates (1954-86,1991-97), minimum tax (1970-78), alternative minimum tax (1979-), income tax surcharges (1968-70), phaseouts of itemized deductions (3% 1991-2005 and 2013, 2% 2006-07, 1% 2008-09) and the 3.8% tax on net investment income (2013). The maximum statutory rate on long-term gains was 28% starting 1991, 20% starting May 1997, 15% starting May 2003 and 20% starting in 2013. The 2008-9 maximum rate includes the effect of the 1% itemized deduction phaseout, computed as 15.35=15+.01*35. Starting 1997, gains on collectibles and certain depreciation recapture are taxed at ordinary rates, up to maximum rates of 28% on collectibles and 25% on recapture. Tax rates changed midyear in 1978, 1981, 1997 and 2003. Estimates are subject to revision.

A Note on Methodology | 169

This level of detail is extremely useful when preparing your tax returns, but confusing when trying to explain the manner in which the basic tax system operates. I chose simplicity.

In addition, I did not address credits. There are numerous credits but I wanted to focus on some of the more egregious shortcomings of the U.S. individual income tax system.

A Note on Methodology

Statistical Appendix

U.S. Individual Income Tax Rates Highest Marginal Rates 1913-2020

Year	Top Rate	Year	Top Rate	Year	Top Rate	Year	Top Rate
1913	7.0%	1940	81.1%	1967	70.0%	1994	39.6%
1914	7.0%	1941	81.0%	1968	75.25%	1995	39.6%
1915	7.0%	1942	88.0%	1969	77.0%	1996	39.6%
1916	15.0%	1943	88.0%	1970	71.75%	1997	39.6%
1917	67.0%	1944	94.0%	1971	70.0%	1998	39.6%
1918	77.0%	1945	94.0%	1972	70.0%	1999	39.6%
1919	73.0%	1946	86.5%	1973	70.0%	2000	39.6%
1920	73.0%	1947	86.5%	1974	70.0%	2001	39.1%
1921	73.0%	1948	82.1%	1975	70.0%	2002	38.6%
1922	58.0%	1949	82.1%	1976	70.0%	2003	35.0%
1923	43.5%	1950	84.36%	1977	70.0%	2004	35.0%
1924	46.0%	1951	91.0%	1978	70.0%	2005	35.0%
1925	25.0%	1952	92.0%	1979	70.0%	2006	35.0%
1926	25.0%	1953	92.0%	1980	70.0%	2007	35.0%
1927	25.0%	1954	91.0%	1981	69.1%	2008	35.0%
1928	25.0%	1955	91.0%	1982	50.0%	2009	35.0%
1929	24.0%	1956	91.0%	1983	50.0%	2010	35.0%
1930	25.0%	1957	91.0%	1984	50.0%	2011	35.0%
1931	25.0%	1958	91.0%	1985	50.0%	2012	35.0%
1932	63.0%	1959	91.0%	1986	50.0%	2013	39.6%
1933	63.0%	1960	91.0%	1987	38.5%	2014	39.6%
1934	63.0%	1961	91.0%	1988	28.0%	2015	39.6%
1935	63.0%	1962	91.0%	1989	28.0%	2016	39.6%
1936	79.0%	1963	91.0%	1990	28.0%	2017	39.6%
1937	79.0%	1964	77.0%	1991	31.0%	2018	37.0%
1938	79.0%	1965	70.0%	1992	31.0%	2019	37.0%
1939	79.0%	1966	70.0%	1993	39.6%	2020	37.0%

Source US Internal Revenue Service, Table 23, 1913 to 2015 see
https://www.irs.gov/statistics/soi-tax-stats-historical-table-23
For 2016 to 2019, see IRS 1040 Instructions

U.S. Individual Income Tax Rates
Lowest Marginal Rates 1913-2020

Year	Low Rate	Year	Low Rate	Year	Low Rate	Year	Low Rate
1913	1.0%	1940	4.4%	1967	14.0%	1994	15.0%
1914	1.0%	1941	10.0%	1968	14.0%	1995	15.0%
1915	1.0%	1942	19.0%	1969	14.0%	1996	15.0%
1916	2.0%	1943	19.0%	1970	14.0%	1997	15.0%
1917	2.0%	1944	23.0%	1971	14.0%	1998	15.0%
1918	6.0%	1945	23.0%	1972	14.0%	1999	15.0%
1919	4.0%	1946	19.0%	1973	14.0%	2000	15.0%
1920	4.0%	1947	19.0%	1974	14.0%	2001	10.0%
1921	4.0%	1948	16.6%	1975	14.0%	2002	10.0%
1922	4.0%	1949	16.6%	1976	14.0%	2003	10.0%
1923	3.0%	1950	17.4%	1977	14.0%	2004	10.0%
1924	1.5%	1951	20.4%	1978	14.0%	2005	10.0%
1925	1.1%	1952	22.2%	1979	14.0%	2006	10.0%
1926	1.1%	1953	22.2%	1980	14.0%	2007	10.0%
1927	1.1%	1954	20.0%	1981	14.0%	2008	10.0%
1928	1.1%	1955	20.0%	1982	12.0%	2009	10.0%
1929	0.4%	1956	20.0%	1983	11.0%	2010	10.0%
1930	1.1%	1957	20.0%	1984	11.0%	2011	10.0%
1931	1.1%	1958	20.0%	1985	11.0%	2012	10.0%
1932	4.0%	1959	20.0%	1986	11.0%	2013	10.0%
1933	4.0%	1960	20.0%	1987	11.0%	2014	10.0%
1934	4.0%	1961	20.0%	1988	15.0%	2015	10.0%
1935	4.0%	1962	20.0%	1989	15.0%	2016	10.0%
1936	4.0%	1963	20.0%	1990	15.0%	2017	10.0%
1937	4.0%	1964	16.0%	1991	15.0%	2018	10.0%
1938	4.0%	1965	14.0%	1992	15.0%	2019	10.0%
1939	4.0%	1966	14.0%	1993	15.0%	2020	10.0%

Source US Internal Revenue Service, Table 23, 1913 to 2015 see
https://www.irs.gov/statistics/soi-tax-stats-historical-table-23
For 2016 to 2019, see IRS 1040 Instructions

Maximum Long Term Capital Gains Tax Rates 1954-2020

Year	Low Rate	Year	Low Rate	Year	Low Rate	Year	Low Rate
1954	25.0%	1971	32.5%	1988	28.0%	2005	15.0%
1955	25.0%	1972	35.0%	1989	28.0%	2006	15.0%
1956	25.0%	1973	35.0%	1990	28.0%	2007	15.0%
1957	25.0%	1974	35.0%	1991	28.0%	2008	15.0%
1958	25.0%	1975	35.0%	1992	28.0%	2009	15.0%
1959	25.0%	1976	28.0%	1993	28.0%	2010	15.0%
1960	25.0%	1977	28.0%	1994	28.0%	2011	15.0%
1961	25.0%	1978	28.0%	1995	28.0%	2012	15.0%
1962	25.0%	1979	28.0%	1996	28.0%	2013	20.0%
1963	25.0%	1980	28.0%	1997	28.0%	2014	20.0%
1964	25.0%	1981	28.0%	1998	20.0%	2015	20.0%
1965	25.0%	1982	20.0%	1999	20.0%	2016	20.0%
1966	25.0%	1983	20.0%	2000	20.0%	2017	20.0%
1967	25.0%	1984	20.0%	2001	20.0%	2018	20.0%
1968	26.9%	1985	20.0%	2002	20.0%	2019	20.0%
1969	27.5%	1986	20.0%	2003	20.0%	2020	20.0%
1970	29.5%	1987	28.0%	2004	15.0%		

Sources:

US Internal Revenue Service, Taxes paid on Long Term Capital Gains, see
https://www.treasury.gov/resource-center/tax-policy/tax-analysis/Documents/Taxes-Paid-on-Long-Term-Capital-Gains.pdf

Tax Policy Center, Taxes Paid on Long Term Capital Gains, May 4, 2017 see
https://www.taxpolicycenter.org/statistics/historical-capital-gains-and-taxes

Statistical Appendix

Bibliography

9th Meeting of the Advisory Expert Group on National Accounts, "Distribution of Income, Consumption and Saving," Agenda Item 12.1, September 8-10, 2014 in Washington, DC.

Americans For Tax Fairness, "Summary of Major Tax Provisions in the Senate and House Coronavirus Stimulus Bills," March 30, 2020.

American Society of Engineers, "2017 Infrastructure Report Card," 2017.

Associated Press

Pail Wiseman, "Behind Virus and Protests: A Chronic US Racial Economic Gap," June 8, 2020.

Josh Boak, "Virus Exposes Sharp Economic Divide: College vs. Non-College," June 6, 2020.

Morrison and Murphy, "Cities Brace for Increasing Unrest, call In National Guard," May 30, 2020.

Groves and Tareen, "Worker Shortage Concerns Loom in Immigration-Heavy Meatpacking," May 26, 2020,

Calvin Woodward, "Coronavirus Shakes the Conceit of American 'Exceptionalism'," April 25, 2020.

Carolyn Thompson, "History, Geography Scores Dip on Nation's Report Card," April 23, 2020.

Dunklin Pritchard, Myers and Fauria, "AP: Publicly Traded Firms Get $365 Million in Small Business Loans," April 21, 2020.

Stafford, Hoyer and Morrison, "Racial Toll of Virus Grows Even more Starker as More Data Emerge," April 18, 2020.

Paul Wiseman, "Virus Exposes US Inequality. Will it Spur Lasting Remedies?" April 12, 2020.

Blomberg Businessweek

"U.S. Corporate Bond Sales Smash Record, Soaring Over $1 Trillion," May 28, 2020.

"Salaries Get Chopped for Many Who Manage to Keep Their Jobs," May 27, 2020.

"Paul Krugman is Pretty Upbeat About the Economy," May 27, 2020,

"Obama Tells Grads Virus Has Torn Back Curtain on Government," May 16, 2020.

"Here are the Companies Getting Federal Covid Relief Funds," April 17, 2020.

"When an Eight-Figure IPO Windfall Can mean a Zero-Digit Tax Bill," June 10, 2019.

"The Wealth Detective Who Finds the Hidden money of the Super Rich," May 23, 2019.

"Here are the Companies Getting Federal COVID Relief Funds," April17, 2020.

"The Tax Law's Big Winner Is The Millionaire CEO," April 12, 2019.

"Piketty's Capital: An Economist's Inequality Ideas Are All the Rage," May 29, 2014.

Board of Governors of the Federal Reserve System, "Changes in U.S. Family Finances from 2010 to 2013: Evidence from the Survey of Consumer Finances," Federal Reserve Bulletin, September 2014, Vol. 100, No. 4.

Board of Trustees, Federal Old-Age and Survivor Insurance and Federal Disability Insurance Trust Funds

"The 2020 Annual Report of the Board of Trustees of the Federal Old-Age and Survivors Insurance and Federal Disability Insurance Trust Funds," April 22, 2020.

"The 2019 Annual Report of the Board of Trustees of the Federal Old-Age and Survivors Insurance and Federal Disability Insurance Trust Funds," April 25, 2019.

The Boards of Trustees, Federal Hospital Insurance and Federal and Federal Supplementary Medical Insurance Trust Funds, "2020 Annual Report of the Boards of Trustees of the Federal Hospital Insurance and

Federal Supplementary Medical Insurance Trust Funds," April 22, 2020.

Boston Consulting Group, "Global Wealth 2016, Navigating the New Client Landscape," June 2016.

Boston 25 News, Drew Karedes, "CDC Review 'Stunning' Universal Testing Results from Boston Homeless Shelter," April 15, 2020.

Brookings

Lauren Bauer, "The COVID-19 Crisis Has Already Left Too Many Children Hungry in America," May 6, 2020.

Henry Aaron, "To Reduce Inequality, Tax Inheritances," November 14, 2019.

William Gale, "Saez and Zucman Say Everything You Knew About Tax Policy is Wrong," October 23, 2019.

Sawhill and Pulliam, "Six Facts About Wealth in the United States," June 25, 2019.

William Gale, "Understanding the Republicans' Corporate Tax Reform," January 10, 2017.

Business Insider, "Chart of the Day: Rich People Really Love to Save Their Money," March 1, 2013.

Center for American Progress, "The Middle-Class Squeeze," September 2014.

Center on Budget and Policy Priorities
- "States Continue to Face Large Shortfalls Due to COVID-19 Effects," June 15, 2020.
- "3 Principles for an Anti-Racist, Equitable State Response to COVID-19 – and a Stronger Recovery," May 21, 2020.
- "Boost the Safety Net to Help People with Fewest Resources Pay for Basics During The Crisis," April 29, 2020.
- "CARES ACT Includes Essential Measures to Respond to Public Health, Economic Crises, But More Will Be Needed," March 27, 2020.
- "Social security Lifts More Americans Above Poverty Than Any Other Program," February 20, 2020.
- "A Guide to Statistics on Historical Trends in Income Inequality," January 13, 2020.
- "Substantial Income of Wealthy Households Escapes Annual Taxation or Enjoys Special Tax Breaks," November 13, 2019.
- "ACA Lawsuit Would Cut Taxes for the Most Well-Off While Ending Health Coverage for Millions," November 4, 2019.
- "State Higher Education Funding Cuts Have Pushed Costs to Students, Worsened Inequality," October 24, 2019.

"How the Federal Tax Code Can Better Advance Racial Equity," July 25, 2019.

"Reducing Cost-of-Living Adjustments Would Make Poverty Line a Less Accurate Measure of Basic Needs," June 11, 2019.

"Learning About the Tax Gap Before Tomorrow's House Hearing," Blog Post, May 8, 2019.

"JCT Estimates: Amended Senate Tax Bill Skewed to Top, Hurts Many Low- and Middle-Income Americans,' November 17, 2017.

"A Guide to Statistics on Historical Trends in Income Inequality," October 11, 2017.

"Understanding Next Week's Census Figures on Poverty and Inequality," September 11, 2014.

"Commentary: Ryan Report Distorts Safety Net's Picture," March 4, 2014.

"What do OECD Data Really Show About U.S. Taxes and Reducing Inequality?" March 12, 2014.

CNBC

Leslie Josephs, "Airline Employees Dilemma: Take Severance or Gamble on Oct. 1 Layoffs," June 10, 2020.

Jeff Cox, "Companies are Ramping Up Share Buybacks, and Their Increasingly Using Debt to Do So," July 30, 2019.

Joseph Stiglitz, "U.S. Does Not Have Capitalism Now: Stiglitz," January 19, 2010.

CNN

Tami Luhby, "US Black-White Inequality in 6 Stark Charts," June 3, 2020.

Michael Linden, "After Two Years, Trump's Tax Cuts Have Failed Americans," December 20, 2019.

Laureen Feiner, "Here's What Bill Gates Thinks about Taxing the Rich," February 12, 2019.

CNN Money, Heather Long, "Inequality in America Keeps Getting Uglier," December 22, 2016.

College Board, "Trends in Student Aid 2019", November 2019.

Conference of the GINI Project, "Income Inequality in Historical and Comparative Perspective," March 2010.

Credit Suisse Research Institute, "Global Wealth Report 2017," November 2017.

Dalio, Ray, "Our Biggest Economic, Social and Political Issue The Two Economies: The Top 40% and the Bottom 60%, LinkedIn Blog, October 23, 2017 see https://www.linkedin.com/pulse/our-biggest-economic-social-political-issue-two-economies-ray-dalio/.

Economic Policy Institute
> Economic Policy Institute and The Center for Popular Democracy, "Still Terrible at Two, The Trump Tax Act Delivered Big Benefits to the Rich and Corporations But Nearly None for Working Families," December, 2019.
>
> "Why America's Workers Need Faster Wage Growth – and What We Do About It." EPI Briefing Paper #382, August 27, 2014.

Financial Times
> African-American Economic Gap Remains Despite Economic Expansion," June 3, 2020.
>
> Foroohar, Rana, "U.S. Inequality, The 'Haves and Have-Mores' in Digital America," August 7, 2017.
>
> Fleming, Sam and Donnan, Shawn, "Middle Class Takes Financial Hit in Most U.S. Cities this Century," May 11, 2016.

Furman, Jason, "Structural Challenges and Opportunities in the U.S. Economy," presentation to the London School of Economics on November 5, 2014.

Global Market Institute at Goldman Sachs, "Savings in America: Building Opportunities for All," Spring 2006.

Harvard Business Review, "Why Stock Buybacks are Dangerous for the Economy, January 7, 2020.

Inequality.org, "Billionaire Bonanza 2020," April 23, 2020.

Institute for Policy Studies

"White Supremacy is the Preexisting Condition: Eight Solutions to Ensure Economic Recovery Reduces the Racial Wealth Divide," June 2020.

"The Case for a Wealth Tax," April 2020.

"Ten Solutions to Bridge the Racial Divide," April 2019.

Institute for Taxation and Economic Policy, "Progressive Revenue-Raising Options", February 2019.

International Bank for Reconstruction and Development Fund

"Global Income Distribution, From the Fall of the Berlin Wall to the Great Recession, Working Paper 6719, December 2013.

"Inequality: A Threat to Economic and Social Development?" April 19, 2012.

Economic Mobility and the Rise of the Latin American Middle Class, 2012.

"Global Inequality, From Class Location to Migrants" working paper 5820, September, 2011.

Bibliography

Attacking the Inequality in the Health Sector, A Synthesis of Evidence and Tools, 2009

"Inequality, Economic Growth and Economic Performance, A Background Note for the World Development Report 2000," 2000.

International Energy Agency, "Sustainable Recovery, World Energy Outlook Special Report," June 2020.

International Monetary Fund

"The Distributional Impact of Recessions: The Global Financial Crisis and the Pandemic Recession," IMF Working Paper WP/20/96, June 2020.

Fiscal Monitor, "Policies to Support People During the COVID-19 Pandemic," April 2020.

Fiscal Monitor, "Tackling Inequality," October 2017.

Global Financial Stability Report, "Markets in the Time of COVID-19," April 2020.

Global Financial Stability Report, "Lower For Longer," October 2019.

IMF Blog, "A New Twist in the Link Between Inequality and Economic Development," Francesco Grigoli, May 11, 2017, see https://blogs.imf.org/2017/05/11/a-new-twist-in-the-link-between-inequality-and-economic-development/

"Income Polarization in the United States," IMF Working Paper W/16/12, June 2016.

"Redistribution, Inequality and Growth," IMF Staff Discussion Paper, February 2014.

"Fiscal Policy and Income Inequality," January 23, 2014, IMF Policy Paper.

"Income Inequality and Fiscal Policy," June 28, 2012, IMF Staff Discussion Paper SDN/12/08.

Finance and Development, "Why Inequality Throws Us Off Balance," 7 articles, September 2011, pages 6-29.

"Inequality and Unsustainable Growth: Two Sides of the Same Coin," April 8, 2011, IMF Staff Discussion Paper SDN/11/08.

Journal of Economic Literature," Inequality and Economic Growth: The Perspective of the New Growth Theories," Volume 37, Number 4, December 1999, pages 1615-1660.

Journal of Political Economy, "Do the Rich Save More?" 2004, Volume 12, pages 397-444.

Journal of Post Keynesian Economics, "Savings and the Distribution of Income," Fall 1991, Volume 14, Number 1, pages 3-22.

Kaiser Family Foundation
> Garfield, Claxton and Levitt, "Eligibility for ACA Health Coverage Following Job Loss", May 13, 2020.
>
> Cubanski, Neuman and Freed, "The Facts on Medicare Spending and Financing," August 2019.

Los Angeles Times
> Karen Kaplan, Six Charts Show How Americans Have Been Affected by COVID-19," June 16, 2020.
>
> Kareem Abdul-Jabbar, "Op-Ed: Don't Understand the Protests? What You're Seeing is People Pushed to the Edge," May 30, 2020.

MarketWatch
> Mike Murphy, "American Airlines to Raise $3.5 Billion in New Financing," June 21, 2020.
>
> Phillip van Doom, "Opinion: Airlines Want a Bailout – But Look How Much They've Spent on Buybacks," March 22, 2020.
>
> Scott Eastman, "This Former Top Obama Official Says One Silver Bullet Would Raise $500 Billion in Personal-Income Tax Plan," November 19, 2019.

Morgan Stanley, "Inequality and Consumption," September 22, 2014.

National Public Radio, "One for the History Books: 14.7% Unemployment, 20.5 Million Jobs Wiped Out," May 8, 2020.

New America, Stephen Burd, "Crisis Point", February 10, 2020.

New York Times

Kurzweil and Wyner, "Rich Kids Are Eating Up the Financial Aid Pot,", June 16, 2020.

Nicholas Kristof, "Crumbs for the Hungry but Windfalls for the Rich," May 23, 2020.

Jeanna Smialek, "Poor American Hit Hardest by Job Losses Amid Lockdowns, Fed Says," May 14, 2020.

Carl Huse, "McConnell Says States Should Consider Bankruptcy, Rebuffing Calls for Aid," April 22, 2020.

David Leonhardt & Yarnya Serkez, "America Will Struggle After Coronavirus. These Charts Show Why," April 10, 2020.

Noam Scheiber, "In a Strong Economy, Why Are So Many Workers on Strike," October 19, 2019.

Emmanuel Saez & Gabriel Zucman, "How to Tax Our Way Back to Justice," October 11, 2019.

Steven Rattner, "A Better Way to Tax the Rich," January 28, 2019.

Cohen, Patricia, "What Could Raising Taxes on the 1% Do? Surprising Amounts," October 16, 2015.

Paul Krugman, "America's Taxation Tradition." March 27, 2014.

Paul Krugman, "Liberty, Equality, Efficiency," March 9, 2014.

Lowrey, Annie, "Incomes Flat in Recovery, but Not for the 1%," February 15, 2013.

New Yorker

Eliza Griswold, "How the Coronavirus is Killing The Middle Class," May 14, 2020.

John Cassidy, "Piketty's Inequality Story in Six Charts, March 26, 2014.

Organization for Economic Cooperation and Development

"A Broken Social Elevator? How to Promote Social Mobility," 2018.

Cingano, Federico, "Trends in Income Inequality and its Impact on Economic Growth," OECD Social, Employment and Migration Working Papers No. 163, 2014.

"Reducing Income Inequality While Boosting Economic Growth: Can It Be Done?" 2012.

"Economic Outlook, Analysis & Forecast: The Equity Implications of Fiscal Consolidation," Economic Outlook Chapter 5, November 2012.

"An Overview of Growing Income Inequalities in OECD Countries: Main Findings," 2011.

"Growing Unequal?: Income Distribution and Poverty in OECD Countries," 2008.

Peterson Institute, Congressional Testimony to the U.S. House Committee on Ways and Means and the U.S. Senate Committee on Finance, "Tax Reform and the Tax Treatment of Debt and Equity," July 13, 2011.

PEW Research Center

Lopez, Raine and Budiman, "Financial and Health Impacts of COVID-19 Vary Widely by Race and Ethnicity," May 5, 2020.

"America's Shrinking Middle Class: A Close Look at Changes Within Metropolitan Areas," May 11, 2016.

"America's Wealth Gap Between Middle-Income and Upper-Income Families is Widest on Record," December, 17, 2014.

"Inequality, Joblessness are Top Threats in 2015, World Economic Forum Expects," November 7, 2014.

"Most See of Household Income and Federal Taxes, 2010," December 2013.

Project Syndicate
> Case and Deaton, "United States of Despair," June 15, 2020.
> Rodrik and Stantcheva, "The Post-Pandemic Social Contract," June 11, 2020.
> Mazzucato and Quaggiotto, "The Big Failure of Small Government," May 19, 2020.
> Marianna Mazzucato, "Capitalism's Triple Threat," March 30, 2020.
> Joseph Stiglitz, "The Truth About the Trump Economy," January 17, 2020.
> Jeffry Sachs, "Why Rich Cities Rebel," October 22, 2019.
> Jayati Ghosh, "The Exploitation Time Bomb," July 16, 2019.
> Michael Spence, "Stock Buybacks are the Wrong Target," February 26, 2019.
> Michael Spence, "How Inequality Undermines Economic Growth," December 26, 2018.
> Angus Deaton, "How Inequality Works," December 21, 2017.
> Joseph Stiglitz, "Deja Voodoo," October 14, 2017.
> Michael Heise, "The Complexity of Inequality," December 9, 2016.
> Michael Spence, "How Inequality Found a Political Voice," October 28, 2016.
> Dambisa Moyo, "The Inequality Puzzle," February 18, 2016.

Foglia, Antonio, "The Invention of Inequality," January 29, 2016.

Qureshi, Zia, "Growing Out of Inequality," Project Syndicate, September 22, 2015.

Rodrik, Dani, "Good and Bad Inequality," Project Syndicate, December 11, 2014.

Joseph Stiglitz, "Inequality and the American Child," December 11, 2014.

Laura Tyson, "The Rising Cost of Inequality," November 30, 2014.

Rodrik, Dani, "How the Rich Rule," Project Syndicate, September 10, 2014.

Edward Wolf, "Inheritance and Inequality," October 21, 2014.

Quantitative Notes, Don Boyd, "A New Synthetic Data Set for Tax Policy Analysis," May 7, 2020, 2020-2.

Quartz, Ephrat Livni, "Congress is Facing Fury over CARES Act Tax Breaks For the Rich," May 8, 2020.

Reuters, "White Houses' Kudlow Floats Cutting Corporate Tax Rate in Half", May 15, 2020.

Saez, Emmanuel

"Striking it Richer: The Evolution of Top Incomes in the United States (Updated with 2012 estimates), September 3, 2013.

"Striking it Richer: The Evolution of Top Incomes in the United States (Updated with 2011 estimates), January 23, 2013.

Saez, Emmanuel and Zucman, Gabriel, "Wealth Inequality in the United States Since 1913: Evidence from Capitalized Income Tax Data," August 2015.

Tax Foundation

"Details and Analysis of Former Vice President Biden's Tax Proposals," April 2020.

"Senate Passes Updated Economic Relief Package [CARES Act} for Individuals and Businesses," March 25, 2020.

"Corporate Tax Rates Around the World, 2019," December 2019.

"Republican Study Committee Budget Contains Important Tax Policy Proposals," May 3, 2019.

"Taxable Income vs. Book Income: Why Some Corporations Pay No Income Tax," May 2, 2019.

"An Overview of Capital Gains Taxes," April 2019.

"Federal Individual Income Tax Rates History, Nominal Dollars 1913-2013," October 17, 2013.

Tax Policy Center

"Historical Highest Marginal Income Tax Rates,", February 4, 2020.

"Effects of the Tax Cuts and Jobs Act: A Preliminary Analysis," June 13, 2018.

"The Effect of the TCJA Individual Income Tax Provisions Across Income Groups and Across The States," March 28, 2018.

"Briefing Book, A Citizen's Guide to the Fascinating Elements of the Federal Tax System," January 2018.

The Economist

"Sovereign Debt Crisis are Coming," May 2020.

"Inequality in America GINI in the Bottle," November 26, 2013.

The Big Picture, Peter Treadway, "Privatize the Gains, Socialize the Losses," February 1, 2010,

The Pew Charitable Trusts, "The Precarious State of Family Balance Sheets, January 2015.

Time

Alana Abramson, "The Real Estate Industry Pushed for $160 Billion in Tax Breaks in the CARES Act, Disclosure Filing Show," May 19, 2019.

Anand Giridharadas, "How America's Elites Lost Their Grip," November 21, 2019.

The Wall Street Journal, "Apple Plans $12 Billion Bond Sale for Buybacks and Dividends," February 16, 2016.

U.S. Bureau of Economic Analysis

"Accounting for the Distribution of Income in the UN National Accounts," November 16, 2012.

"Economic Inequality," July 2015.

"Income and Poverty in the United States: 2013," Current Population Reports, September 2014.

U.S. Congressional Budget Office,

"The Budgetary Effects of Laws Enacted In Response to the 2020 Corona Pandemic, March and April 2020," June 11, 2020.

"CBO's Current Projection of Output, Employment and Interest Rates and a Preliminary Look at Federal Deficits for 2020 and 2021," April 24, 2020.

"Federal Budget in 2019," April 15, 2020.

"Preliminary Estimate of the Effects of H.R. 748, the CARES Act, Public Law 116-136," April 16, 2020.

"Federal Debt: A Primer," March 2020.

"The Distribution of Household Income, 2016," July, 2019.

Bibliography | 195

"The Economic Effects of the 2017 Tax Revision: Preliminary Observations," R45736, May 22, 2019.

"Health Insurance Coverage for People under Age 65: Definitions and Estimates for 2015 to 2018," April 2019.

"CBO Confirms GOP Tax Law Contributes to Darkening Fiscal Future,", February 5, 2019.

"Marginal Federal Tax Rates on Labor Income: 1962 to 2028," January 2019.

"Options for reducing the Deficits: 2019 to 2028," December 2018.

"Allocating State and Local Taxes to U.S. Households," presentation to the National Tax Association's 111th Annual Conference on Taxation, New Orleans, LA, November 17, 2018.

"The Distribution of Household Income, 2015," November, 2018.

"Capital Gains Taxes: An Overview," March 16, 2018.

"Trends in the Distribution of Household Income," presentation at the University of Michigan's 65th Annual Economic Outlook Conference, November 16, 2017.

"Effective Marginal Tax Rates for Low- and Moderate-Income Workers in 2016," Panel organized by the Department of Health and Human Services, Office of the Assistance Secretary for Planning and Evaluation, and the Institute of Research on Poverty at the University of Wisconsin, June 26, 2018.

"International Comparison of Corporate Income Tax Rates," March 2017.

"Trends in Family Wealth: 1989 to 2013," August 2016.

"Trends in Family Wealth, 1989 to 2013," August 2016.

"The Distribution of Household Income and Federal Taxes 2013," June 2016.

"The Distribution of Household Income and Federal Taxes 2011," November 2014.

"The Distribution of Household Income and Federal Taxes 2010," December 2013.

"Changes in CBO's Baseline Projections Since January 2001," June 7, 2012.

"Trends in the Distribution of Household Income Between 1979 and 2007, October 2011.

"Effects of the 1981 Tax Act on the Distribution of Income and Taxes Paid," August 1986.

U.S. Congressional Budget Office and the Joint Committee on Taxation, "The Distribution of

Asset Holdings and Capital Gains," August 2016.

U.S. Congressional Research Service
"Individual Income Tax Rates and Other Key Elements of the Federal Individual Income Tax: 1988 to 2019 Tax Years," RL34498, Updated February 8, 2019.

"Capital Gains Taxes: An Overview," 96-769, March 16, 2018.

"The Economic Effects of Capital Gains Taxation," R40411, June 18, 2010.

U.S. Department of Health and Human Services, "2015 Actuarial Report on the Financial Outlook for Medicaid," 2015.

U.S. Department of Treasury, "Taxes Paid on Long-Term Capital Gains, 1977-2014, December 20, 2016.

U.S. Government Accountability Office,
"Marginal Federal Tax Rates on Labor Income: 1962 to 2018," January 2019.

"Corporate Income Taxes, Most Large Profitable U.S. Corporations Paid Tax but Effective Tax Rates Differed Significantly from the Statutory Rate," GAO-16-363, March 2016.

"Retirement Security, Most Households Approaching Retirement Have Low Savings," GAO-15-419, May 2015.

"Corporate Income Taxes, Effective Tax Rates Can Differ Significantly from the Statutory Rate," GAO-13-520, May 2013.

U.S. Internal Revenue Service

"Business Expenses 2019," Publication 535.

"Business Expenses 2015," Publication 535.

"Instructions for Form 4626, Alternative Minimum Tax – Corporations, 2015"

"Instruction for Form 6251, Alternative Minimum Tax – Individuals, 2015"

"Investment Income and Expenses (Including Capital Gains and Losses) 2018," Publication 550.

"Investment Income and Expenses (Including Capital Gains and Losses 2015," Publication 550.

"Social Security and Equivalent Railroad Retirement Benefits 2019," Publication 915.

"Social Security and Equivalent Railroad Retirement Benefits 2015," Publication 915.

"Survivor, Executors and Administrators 2019," Publication 559.

"Survivor, Executors and Administrators 2015," Publication 559.

"Tax Reform, Basics for Individuals and Families, Tax Year 2019," Publication 5307.

"Tax Reform, What's New For Your Business, Tax Year 2018," Publication 5318.

"Your Federal Income Tax, 2019 Tax Guide," Publication 17.

"Your Federal Income Tax, 2015 Tax Guide," Publication 17.

U.S. Joint Committee on Taxation,

"Description of the Tax Provisions of Public Law 116-136, the Coronavirus Aid, Relief, and Economic Security ('CARES') Act, April 23, 2020.

Letter to Senators Whitehouse and Doggett, from Thomas Barthold regarding distributional effects of reducing the time limits on corporate losses under CARES, April 9, 2020.

"Overview of the Federal Tax System as in Effect for 2018," February 7, 2018.

"Distribution Effects of the Chairman's Modification to the Chairman's Mark of the 'Tax Cuts and Jobs Act,' Scheduled for Markup by the Committee on Finance on November 15, 2017," November 17, 2017.

U.S. Constitution.

USA Today, "4 Coronavirus Stimulus Packages. $2.4 trillion in Funding. See what that means to the National Debt," May 8, 2020.

Washington Post

Dana Milbank, "Forget Vaccines and Treatments. The Very Stable Genius has Foolproof Coronavirus Cure," June 16, 2020.

Christopher Ingraham, "Racial Inequality in Minneapolis is Among the Worst in the Nation, "May 30, 2020.

Zapatosky and Stanley-Blacker, "Gripped By Disease, Unemployment and Outrage at the Police, American Plunges Into Crisis," May 29, 2020.

Tara Isabella Burton, "Billionaires are Playing Savior Now. But They Broke the Economy to Begin With," May 15, 2020.

Abelson, Priest, Sullivan and Dungca, "Boom-and-Bust Federal Funding After 9/11 Undercut Hospital Preparedness for Pandemics," May 2, 2020.

O'Connell, Rich and Whoriskey, "Public Companies Received $1 Billion in Stimulus Funds Meant for Small Businesses," May 1, 2020.

Bibliography | 201

Dana Milbank, "Trump and Kushner Could Reap a Pandemic Windfall," April 14, 2020.

Kessler, Rizzo and Cahlan, "Fact-Checking Donald Trump's State of the Union Address," February 4, 2020.

"Economic Mobility Hasn't Changed in a Half-century in America, Economists Declare," January 23, 2014.

World Economic Forum, "The Global Social Mobility Report 2020, Equality, Opportunity and a New Economic Imperative," January 19, 2020.

Yardeni Research, Yardeni, Abbott and Quintana, "Stock market Indicators: A&P 500 Buybacks & Dividends," July 31, 2019.

Bibliography

Acknowledgements

Special thanks to my Analytical Consultant Beth Jarosz who helped a great deal with the data and the analysis. Thanks also go to my Editor, Patricia Rice who improved the readability of this book.

www.ingramcontent.com/pod-product-compliance
Lightning Source LLC
Chambersburg PA
CBHW060832220526
45466CB00003B/1079